The Last of the 357th Infantry

Expand your library with other titles from Regnery History's World War II Collection

40 Thieves on Saipan: The Elite Marine Scout-Snipers in One of WWII's Bloodiest Battles
by Joseph Tachovsky with Cynthia Kraack

Coffin Corner Boys: One Bomber, Ten Men, and Their Harrowing Escape from Nazi-Occupied France
by Carole Engle Avriett

Fatal Dive: Solving the World War II Mystery of the USS Grunion
by Peter F. Stevens

Fierce Valor: The True Story of Ronald Speirs and His Band of Brothers
by Jared Frederick and Erik Dorr

Forgotten Fifteenth: The Daring Airmen Who Crippled Hitler's War Machine
by Barrett Tillman

Lost Airmen: The Epic Rescue of WWII U.S. Bomber Crews Stranded behind Enemy Lines
by Charles Stanley Jr.

Marine Raiders: The True Story of the Legendary WWII Battalions
by Carole Engle Avriett

Operation Snow: How a Soviet Mole in FDR's White House Triggered Pearl Harbor
by John Koster

Saving My Enemy: How Two WWII Soldiers Fought Against Each Other and Later Forged a Friendship That Saved Their Lives
by Bob Welch

Soaring to Glory: A Tuskegee Airman's Firsthand Account of World War II
by Philip Handleman with Lt. Col. Harry T. Stewart Jr.

Target Patton: The Plot to Assassinate General George S. Patton
by Robert K. Wilcox

The General and the Genius: Groves and Oppenheimer—The Unlikely Partnership That Built the Atom Bomb
by James Kunetka

The Hidden Nazi: The Untold Story of America's Deal with the Devil
by Dean Reuter, Colm Lowery, and Keith Chester

The Hunt for Hitler's Warship
by Patrick Bishop

The Last Fighter Pilot: The True Story of the Final Combat Mission of World War II
by Don Brown with Captain Jerry Yellin

The Last of the 357th Infantry: Harold Frank's WWII Story of Faith and Courage
by Mark Hager

The Price of Valor: The Life of Audie Murphy, America's Most Decorated Hero of World War II
by David A. Smith

The Rifle: Combat Stories from America's Last WWII Veterans, Told through an M1 Garand
by Andrew Biggio

www.RegneryHistory.com

MARK HAGER

THE LAST
of the
357th INFANTRY

ᚷ

HAROLD FRANK'S WWII STORY
OF FAITH *and* COURAGE

REGNERY
HISTORY
Washington, D.C.

Unless otherwise noted, all photographs courtesy of Forks of the Yadkin and Davie County History Museum Inc.

Regnery History™ is a trademark of Salem Communications Holding Corporation
Regnery® is a registered trademark and its colophon is a trademark of Salem Communications Holding Corporation

Cataloging-in-Publication data on file with the Library of Congress

ISBN: 978-1-68451-404-5
Library of Congress Control Number: 2021952741

First trade paperback edition published 2023

Published in the United States by
Regnery History, an Imprint of
Regnery Publishing
A Division of Salem Media Group
Washington, D.C.
www.RegneryHistory.com

Manufactured in the United States of America

10 9 8 7 6 5 4 3 2 1

Books are available in quantity for promotional or premium use. For information on discounts and terms, please visit our website: www.Regnery.com.

Dedicated to Lou Hager

"A mother in the finest word imaginable."
—Mark Hager

CONTENTS

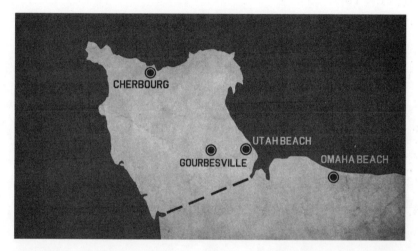

Normandy—Cherbourg. *Courtesy of Brannon Judd and Pritchett Cotten*

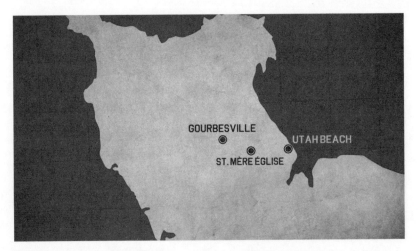

Normandy—Sainte Mère Église. *Courtesy of Brannon Judd and Pritchett Cotten*

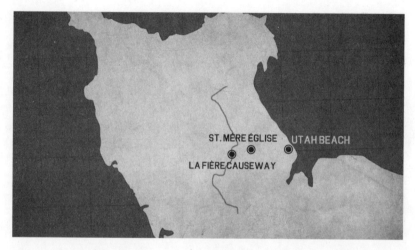

Normandy—La Fière Causeway. *Courtesy of Brannon Judd and Pritchett Cotten*

Foreword

When I was growing up in rural North Carolina during the 1970s and '80s, I customarily met veterans from both World War II and Korea. Many veterans were reluctant to discuss their war experiences. I considered myself lucky when they felt comfortable enough to talk about it. I learned to be patient, especially with an uncle who was a decorated World War II veteran who served with the U.S. 1st Armored Division in both the African and Italian Campaigns. He survived the Battle of Anzio but was severely injured during a fight against German Tiger tanks. He drove a tank that was destroyed by a Mark VI Tiger. He was knocked unconscious but awakened to the sight of all his combat crew members dead and body parts scattered everywhere. The war affected him all his life, and sadly, I helped bury him in western North Carolina, Christmas of 2018. One of my cousins served in the Navy as a sailor aboard the USS *Pennsylvania* during the Japanese attack on Pearl Harbor. Thankfully, he managed to document his story with a video interview following a family reunion. Most of the stories I heard from veterans centered upon theaters of action, weapons, and the units they served under. Early in my career, I became a veteran after volunteering for the U.S. Army during the 1980s. While serving as a U.S. Army field artillery surveyor, I witnessed the Cold War and the Soviet Union's attempt to force communism upon Western Europe. I walked some of the battlefields of both world wars and became a scholar of U.S. military history. It didn't take long to understand that freedom is never cheap. Plus I knew that the veterans of World War II were exceptional and deserved special examination.

Based on my military experience, several years of historic reenacting, and collegiate work in public history, I developed a unique perspective on military historiography. I felt tasked to write a book that could be used by students and novice historians to better define and understand the soldiers of the Greatest Generation. Central questions I wanted to answer included: What made the American soldier of World War II one of the most resourceful and productive soldiers in world history? Furthermore, how can I memorialize veterans who lived during the worldwide depression? The U.S. military was underfunded, lacked resources, and was vastly undermanned. So how, when given the task to defend freedom, did some of these veterans choose service before finishing high school? The forces that aligned against them in 1941 were dark and overwhelming.

I hope the readers of Harold Frank's story understand that a weapon is no better than the soldier whom it equips. Contrast that with the survivability of a combat veteran. Survivability was due to a combination of military training, childhood upbringing, environmental factors, and faith in God. Adaptability to change, whether environmental or physical, is difficult to train in most military recruits. Living through the Great Depression produced a generation of Americans used to rugged conditions at home. They had to find adaptive and innovative ways to survive in an environment filled with unemployment, low wages, consumer debt, agricultural struggles due to drought, dropping food prices, and banks unable to liquidate loans. In spite of these hard times it became necessary to prepare for America's entry into World War II. Volunteers were recruited to join our military. We also needed a workforce capable of producing munitions, armaments, and other supplies. Factories and industrial resources in shipbuilding, aircraft, cars, and tanks contributed substantially to the war effort. So did the Americans who built them. Overall, American ingenuity burst forth from the generation of people who lived in the Great Depression. This diversity and what it meant to step up in our country's time of need was embedded in our veterans of World War II. The world recognized such soldiers as a type: the American combat soldier.

Presenting the story of Harold Frank became a real challenge requiring a more expansive approach to historiography. Years of university studies, research, and work in public history were beneficial for investigating military experience in a way that I call "ground truthing." In other words, will the reader be equipped to understand the struggle a veteran endures in combat? Also, Harold Frank's story draws an additional element of what it was like to be a POW in Nazi Germany. The treatment of U.S. POWs by both German and Japanese forces is well documented. Atrocities were numerous, with starvation and executions a stark commonalty. While interviewing Harold Frank in the discovery phase, all battles, weapons, and units were investigated through sources ranging from Normandy, France; Fort Bragg, North Carolina; the National Museum of the Mighty Eighth Air Force, Savannah, Georgia; the National D-Day Museum (now the National WWII Museum) in New Orleans; and various secondary written sources. The process clearly revealed that the survival of Harold Frank bordered more on miraculous than just extraordinary circumstances. Case in point was the collision course that Allied soldiers faced after D-Day on the Cotentin Peninsula of France.

The Cotentin Peninsula and its important port at Cherbourg became a matter of importance to hold at all costs for both German and Allied forces. The 357th Infantry was given the audacious task of blocking movements of the German Army either retreating from or attempting to reinforce Cherbourg. The result was an intense struggle in daily combat without reprieve for several months, ending in the battles of Gourbesville, Hill 122, Beaucoudray, and Saint-Lô. The regiment suffered horrendous losses and multiple companies were virtually destroyed. Harold Frank served in the U.S. 2nd Battalion, Company G of the 357th Infantry which landed on Utah Beach, June 8, 1944 (D-Day+2). His battalion met heavy resistance as they attempted to relieve isolated pockets of the 101st and 82nd Airborne units operating in and around the Merderet River Bridge. A month later Harold Frank, being the last experienced BAR rifleman in the 357th, led a night patrol to find two lost U.S. infantry companies. Simultaneously the 15th German Parachute Regiment launched a massive counterattack catching the exposed patrol. Although wounded, Harold Frank and four others fought for nine hours and diverted enough attention to blunt the German offensive. Harold Frank survived but was captured. He endured and survived a ten-month POW experience that many of his compatriots succumbed to.

The location of the POW work camp was adjacent to Dresden, which placed Harold Frank on another collision course with a thousand-plane firebombing of that city that commenced in the predawn hours of February 13, 1945, followed by two more air attacks on April 17, 1945. The survivors joined tens of thousands of civilians and other POWs forced to flee from Russian military advancements along the Eastern Front moving towards Berlin. We all can learn from these moments in history. Harold Frank was lucky that his survival skills started developing as a young child. The U.S. Army trained him for many challenging situations but so did his family and the Great Depression.

The Great Depression taught him to respond to circumstances in several ways. "Waste not, want not" was the unwritten code for Frank, his family, and many other families across America during this time. Enduring hardships, an intense work ethic, family support, and the love of God shaped him to be a combat soldier and the man he is today. His survival can be attributed to all of these elements. The secret to his and other veterans' survivals in World War II was largely the product of what has been called "The Greatest Generation." It is this generation that bore witness to the effects of the Great Depression and, after World War II's end, America's own rise to become a victorious superpower.

The Great Depression came to an end when America entered World War II to fight with Allied forces against Germany, Italy, and Japan in 1941. This entry required about sixteen million young recruits to serve. Thus, America's war effort created the increased need for production and full employment which ended the Depression. Relatives and friends also contributed their own thoughts and struggles to the occasional dialog about the Great Depression. It's my impression that many authors of World War II history leave out the impact of the Depression from military historiography. Therefore, the first five chapters of this account are dedicated to Depression-era life, which is necessary to understand life then and today.

When I teach university students and talk to young people in the community about life during the Depression, I've found that they have a lack of knowledge on the subject. So obviously I feel the need to teach and preserve some of the thoughts and observations of Americans living during the Depression and especially those of the combat soldiers from the Greatest Generation. Inadvertently lost or lacking in military historiography are the life and hardships that shaped not just Harold Frank but countless soldiers of this time.

The United States since the Great Depression and World War II has done well despite many struggles economically and the forthcoming "Cold War" on communism that lasted over four decades. Today the U.S. military is dependent upon volunteers trained to defend against any potential two-front war. Less than 2 percent of American families are directly involved in the U.S. military despite being in a war against "radical Islamic terrorists" since 2001. Perhaps that is why current conflicts in foreign nations seem to generate so little concern in students whom I teach and talk with during the school year.

Comically, terms common to the Depression are now foreign to the current generation. For instance, cooking with "lard" or making "lye soap" are as alien as both the "outhouse" and the "smokehouse." Imagine attempting to explain the operations needed to keep up a "wood cookstove" and keep butter and milk fresh in either a "springhouse" or "icebox?" The few Depression alumni I still know are well into their 90s. They will smile when people today become concerned about severe weather and ask, "What will we do if the power goes out for several days?" These alumni may point to an antique kerosene, a candle lantern, or a woodstove and say, "That's all the power you need."

Following the attack on Pearl Harbor, America reacted in a determination best illustrated by the quote of Japanese Admiral

Isoroku Yamamoto who feared that a "sleeping giant" had just been awakened. Moreover, the reader of the Harold Frank's story will end up with not just a history of warfare during World War II, but a clear understanding of the resourcefulness, determination and faith packaged into men accustomed to hardship before being called into action. Nearly four years after Pearl Harbor, and against incredible odds, the Axis powers were destroyed, and America emerged as the champion of freedom and liberty. America did awaken quickly to build an industrial complex from scrap, which in four years rose from nothing to defeat two superpowers while utilizing young soldiers with minimal education.

The major challenge I had was documenting Harold Frank's combat experience. I knew discussing combat can be difficult for veterans. Under the constraints of patience and appropriateness, it became obvious when to end the conversation. Harold refused to tell his wife Reba about the war, although sometimes he brought up events that sparked lots of emotion. Thus, after sixty years of marriage, Harold had successfully shut down memories of combat horror. On several occasions when conversation triggered a lost memory, Harold would sadly say, "I'll have nightmares of this tonight." How the horror of fighting during World War II compared to other conflicts is better understood through the explanation of a close friend and combat veteran, Command Sergeant Major Clinton Murray of the 82nd Airborne Division. He described veterans like Harold as, "Soldiers that lived, slept, and fought from a small, two-man foxhole. That meager circumstance continued for many months and years. They seldom had a chance to shower or recover in a barracks environment. Every day was a challenge. [During World War II] the war with weather was horrendous; below zero temperatures, intense snow, heavy rain or heat all required environmental adaptation and had to be defeated. The soldiers that landed in Normandy could be traced across Europe foxhole to foxhole. That by itself is incredible." That leads me to the main problem of documenting the day-to-day story of a veteran who had blocked off much of his memory.

In 1973 a fire broke out in a warehouse holding National World War II records. Sadly, many of the Normandy records went up with the smoke. After his wife's death, Harold reluctantly gave in to a request to tell some of his story to Mike Barnhardt, who is the editor for the *Davie County Enterprise Record* newspaper. The stories by this time were quite scattered and dates unsure. I came on the scene a few months later, and I determined to put back the pieces. Harold knew and explained that he came in on Utah Beach but wasn't with the first wave. In a solemn tone he explained that he was a replacement for someone with a similar BAR rifle who lost his life. Harold had a small paperback history book of the 357th Infantry which stated that some of the combat soldiers came in late on June 6, 1944, but the bulk of the unit entered combat on June 10, 1944, outside of Sainte Mère Église and toward Gourbesville. Harold's official Army paperwork listed the date of his Combat Infantry Badge, or CIB, as June 10, 1944. He guessed he must have arrived during that time span. There is a replacement list calling out Harold and his BAR assistant gunner Paul Esworthy which documents the two in Gourbesville on June 15, 1944. Added to this was his conviction that he had slept two nights near Utah beach before he entered combat. Thanks to Sylvain Kast, a World War II military historian and tour guide in Normandy, Harold was able to piece the story together and finally have closure.

It's difficult for civilians and most family members of loved ones who served to comprehend the extent to which a combat veteran will endeavor to erase the horrors of war. As a veteran myself, I am very cautious and guarded in how I help them recall their war stories. Veterans understand this, and I would caution anyone trying to pry into "Dad's combat story." James Deal from Faith, North Carolina, was a close friend of Harold Frank and a fellow World War II combat veteran who fought with the 737th Tank Battalion of the 35th Infantry Division under General Patton. While sitting next to Harold, Deal once told me, "I never knew the town I fought through, or village, or road, or day and date! I didn't care to know, or ever remember. I just wanted to protect my tank and men. Most of all, I wanted to come home and see my family. Historians can write and tell me everything, but they don't know everything, and never will. Combat is confusing and difficult to describe. Just depending upon a paper written by someone afterwards does nothing, because they weren't there and definitely not with us."

Harold Frank's story has already impacted many. I spoke about Harold Frank in the fall of 2017 near Lexington, North Carolina, to a large group of veterans who had gathered at the

NASCAR race shop of Richard Childress, the owner of Richard Childress Racing. In addition, I showed a short documentary I had completed earlier that summer. Harold Frank was an inspiration to those veterans and to Richard Childress, who had become a good friend to Harold Frank. Upon hearing of this book, Childress wanted to add these words:

> Harold Frank is an American Hero and an icon in our community. I've known him for many years and have admired him for his commitment to our local veterans and his willingness to share his story as a POW. Harold came to speak to my employees at Richard Childress Racing in 2015 at our annual kickoff lunch and we all left feeling stronger, more hopeful and most of all, more appreciative of our veterans. Harold represents the millions of servicemen and women that have served admirably, did what they were told, and didn't seek recognition for it. He truly does come from the "greatest generation." His story of resiliency while a POW is something that we should all hear and learn from.

> What I admire most about Harold is his love for his neighbors and fellow veterans. He's always willing to lend an ear and is very active with local veteran events. Harold is a frequent visitor of our monthly "Veterans Coffee" event at Richard Childress Racing the first Wednesday of every month. He rarely misses

the Veterans Coffee and always has a warm smile and a willingness to fellowship.

I'm honored to know Harold Frank and feel indebted to him for his service and sacrifice to our great nation during World War II.

I hope you enjoy the Harold Frank Story. Most of all, remember all those who fought to give the hope of freedom and liberty.

—Mark Hager

CHAPTER 1

The Construction of a Man

On a cold Monday morning in March of 1929 at 4:00, Harold Frank, just five years old, was awakened. Edward walked to Harold's bed and gently shook Harold's shoulder.

"Son, get up, let's get started."

"Okay, Daddy," Harold said.

Harold rose from his straw tick bed made from last year's thrashed-wheat straw tightly packed through an opening along the center of a heavy denim cloth. He slipped out from underneath three homemade quilts made from feed sacks and old clothing. Only the face of the quilt showed designed squares. Harold dressed in a blue, long-sleeved shirt and bib overalls before donning his "hand-me-down jacket" that came from his older cousin Homer Penniger. He quickly grabbed his slingshot, which he always carried for hunting small game. Harold's seven-year-old sister Naomi was in grade school, and he could

Naomi Frank with her first child, late 1940s

hear her already in the kitchen helping their mother Annie prepare breakfast from the wood cookstove. Annie grabbed wood
from the woodbox next to the stove. Then she placed it in the
stove and lit the wood with a pine knot and matches. The stove
was heated and ready after thirty minutes. While it was heating,
Annie went to the smokehouse to cut ham and gather eggs from
the chicken house—a mere one hundred feet from the smokehouse. Each meal required one and a half hours to cook, with
dinner demanding the most time. Harold was born on September 30, 1924. Although two years younger than Naomi, he
was expected to learn farm life quickly. By ten years of age,

Naomi knew how to cook biscuits and gravy, dress a chicken, keep up the house, wash clothes on a washboard, and out pick Harold in the cotton field. It wasn't a contest or a forced-labor program. It was the Great Depression, and the survival of the Frank family was dependent upon each family member's contribution. There was no time for the weary of heart, much less self-pity, and there was definitely no room for complaining.

Annie, standing in the kitchen, said, "Son, eat a good meal 'cause you won't be getting much for supper." The farm provided a substantive life for the family and in this case, the work needs demanded an increase in caloric intake. To Harold, the smell of fried eggs, ham, biscuits, and red-eye gravy was a delight. They had milk fresh from the farm to drink, and it was kept cool in the icebox sitting on the back porch. A hundred-pound half block of ice delivered weekly by truck kept the milk, butter, cream, and some meat cool.

In a few minutes, they had eaten, and Edward looked at Harold and said, "Let's go son. Let's get the horse teams together." They went to the barn and let the Frank family's three thoroughbred horses and a mule feed on corn, oats, and hay provided by the Frank farm. Edward owned only one of the thoroughbred horses. His was named Zeb. Uncle Grady owned the mule named Henry, and Uncle Paul owned the other two thoroughbreds, whose names were Nellie and Gray. A few minutes later they pulled each horse one at a time from his stall.

Edward placed the bridle on first, beginning by putting the bit in the mouth before pulling the bridle over the ears and fastening it to the throatlatch holding the bridle. Edward put the collar around the neck. The hames fastened to the collar, which then fed the coupling harness back to the wagon and then connected the harness to the doubletree. The five-foot-wide doubletree had a ring on both ends and was connected to the tongue of the wagon. Each line of the collar was then connected to each horse. Harold held the check line tightly while Edward finished connecting the teams to the wagon.

By 5:00 a.m. all connections were made, so Edward and Harold jumped on the lead wagon. The lead horse team was pulled by Zeb and Henry, and the second team was pulled by Nellie and Gray, who were tied to the back of the lead team's wagon. Edward's eldest brother, Uncle Grady, was already at the timber mill site milling timber. Edward was impressed with Harold, who was only five years old, and said, "You think you can handle the horse teams alone by the time you're eight?"

"Yes, sir!" Harold replied.

The sawmill the two brothers operated consisted of a circle saw powered by a 10–20 McCormick-Deering tractor, which had been purchased by the Frank family before the Depression. The motor was powered via a hand crank fueled by kerosene. The rough timber, once milled, would then be loaded into each wagon, with the lead team's wagon being filled with milled lumber first before the second team was brought up and loaded.

The two men and Harold made two loads per day and then returned to complete unfinished chores on the farm. Harold helped by bringing in fresh water from Grandpa Billy's well near where the timber was cut. He also took lunch (consisting of ham sandwiches that Harold's mom had prepared before they left) to the men. Harold also brought up each of the horse teams close to the mill site, and Edward and Uncle Grady loaded the milled lumber.

On Tuesday, April 9, Edward and Harold left earlier than usual in a push to possibly make three loads in a day. The wagon teams approached Grandpa Billy's house, and as they passed, Edward suddenly stopped the horse team, pointed to the smoke-house, and gave the reins to Harold while yelling, "Son, here hold the team. The smokehouse door is open." Edward looked at Grandpa Billy's house and said to Harold, "I don't see a light on in the house. Stay here and hold the teams."

Edward quietly pulled out his 12-gauge shot gun and walked up the steps to the house. He knocked on the door and awakened Grandpa. Edward and Grandpa Billy, armed with shotguns, walked to the smokehouse. Edward entered and after a few seconds reported, "Someone has stolen three sacks of cured meat."

The two men spread out and checked the other structures, circling the horse teams then signaling to each other that all was secure as they walked back. As the two men returned to the teams, Harold overheard Grandpa Billy state, "If I'd a caught them I'd would've shot them. This is all the meat I have. Three hooks is half a hog!"

"Well," said Edward, "whoever it was either came last evening when they knew you were asleep or we just stopped them from taking all the meat."

Harold looked up at Grandpa Billy and asked, "Grandpa would you of shot him in the legs to keep from killing him?"

Grandpa Billy responded in anger and replied, "If he was walking on his hands!" And pointing at the smokehouse he said, "That's all the meat I have, and it took a lot of work to get that."

The culprits were long gone. Edward took control of the teams and looked at Grandpa Billy and then back at Harold before he said, "We've got work to do and Grady will be waiting." Thus began another full day at the mill site.

By May, the milled timber needed to construct the two houses had made it home. A neighbor had a planer to dress and finish the lumber before framing the house. After the wood had been milled, dressed, and unloaded at the new home locations, the old homes were rolled back from their foundations. Using house jacks and spare timber from a local mill in Linwood, North Carolina, the old homes were removed from their foundations. Edward's resourcefulness caught Harold's attention as he was trying to understand how they would move the homes. The timber came from a veneer plant that had some old rollers, each about eight feet long, which were made from cores of popular trees and used to create the veneer. When each log was cut to the very core—that is, down to about six inches in diameter—they were discarded. Edward and Uncle Grady picked up a wagon load of thirty-six rollers. Together with the jacks, each of the homes was lifted carefully and moved from each foundation to about one hundred fifty feet away.

The new houses were then constructed, with Uncle Grady's house completed first in the summer of 1930, followed by

Children of Grandpa Bill Frank—Edward, Annias, Dela, Grady, Iris, Grace, Bessie, Mary, and Paul

Edward's house in the summer of 1931. Neither house was insulated or equipped with indoor plumbing. The heat was supplied by two fireplaces: one in the front room and the other in the living room, with a flue for the wood cookstove in the kitchen. Edward's house had six rooms, two halls, and a porch that wrapped around the house. The effort Edward and Uncle Grady put in each day to cut the timber, mill it, and build their homes left a lifelong impression upon Harold of their hard work and attention to detail.

The new homes featured a slightly larger kitchen that made the weekly Saturday bath easier. Using the water reservoir on

Frank home built by Edward and Harold

the wood cookstove, the water was heated, usually in conjunction with Saturday dinner. When dinner was over and the kitchen cleared, a washtub hanging in the nearby shed was brought in. The kitchen doors were closed, and the shade was pulled down over the window. Then, the heated water was poured into the wash tub set. Each family member took turns taking a bath, getting dressed, removing the bath water, dumping it out, and then replacing it with fresh warm water from the cookstove reservoir. After bathing was completed, the tub was removed, washed out, and hung to dry on the back fence to await use a week later.

In the early summer of 1931, Harold went hunting with his slingshot whenever he had spare time. While walking in the yard, Harold heard his Grandpa Billy yell, "Boy, bring me a brick to lay my head on." Grandpa Billy would visit, and on a sunny day he sat under the shade of a sugar maple tree between the two new homes.

Harold saw him under the sugar maple and said, "Let me go and get you a pillow."

"No! I don't want a pillow. I want a brick," Grandpa Billy replied.

Harold saw Annie and exclaimed, "Grandpa wants a brick. Shouldn't I bring a pillow?"

Annie laughed and said, "He wants a brick, so get him one."

Harold found a brick in the leftover brick pile from the house construction and took it to him. After a minute, Grandpa Billy was sound asleep. Such was a glimpse of daily life during the Depression.

CHAPTER 2

"Save Everything but the Squeal"

E ach morning on the Frank farm, Harold would wake and gather the slop jar or chamber pot—which was the size of a ten-quart bucket with a porcelain lid. He would take it to the outhouse situated two hundred feet between the house and the horse barn. There he emptied the waste and washed out the slop jar near the horse trough. Harold's next chores were to milk two cows and haul back fresh water from the well, which was situated off the right corner of the house. He drew the water from a windlass that held the small bucket and pulley. He poured this smaller bucket into a ten-quart water bucket. Harold had to bring in three water buckets to provide the day's water needs. Afterwards Harold had to fill up the wood cookstove box and water reservoir. During the fall, Harold and his little brother Archie would cut popular and pine planks roughly one foot long and stack them for the spring. In March and April after the wood was seasoned, they split it into kindling one and a half inches wide and a foot long for Annie to use in the stove. Little did Harold know that this activity would one day serve him well as a soldier in World War II. After she finished cooking, Annie dumped the ashes, and Harold would fill the kindling box back up to be ready for dinner and supper cooking. After school Harold refilled any wood, then milked the cows in the evening. He brought back the slop jar and placed it under the bed.

The Frank family was schooled in all aspects of farming, cutting timber, and operating a sawmill. The churning for butter and cream was a weekly chore directed by Annie. When Harold turned eight, he graduated from hoeing the crops to running the three-foot cultivator pulled by Zeb. He plowed all day with a one-and-a-half-hour rest for dinner when Annie would signal the noon time meal was ready by ringing the outside bell. Harold watered the horse and sometimes drank from the same horse trough. Then he put Zeb in the stable to feed on Lespedeza, a common grain raised on the farm for feed and also primarily as a source of cover and food for quail. It was stored for the horses away from the feed box. Afterwards, Harold washed the sweat and grime of the fields away and came in for the big meal of the day, dinner.

After eating, Harold and Naomi helped Annie clear the table, and Edward would nap for the final thirty minutes of the midday rest, giving both man and horse a break during the heat of the day. Plowing resumed and lasted till evening. Before resting, the men had to unhook the horse teams, place more feed, and clean up. The main income of the Frank family was a cash crop of sweet potatoes and cotton. Standard crops such as corn and a variety of beans were grown and canned for the winter. Cabbage was cultivated and turned into kraut. Grains including wheat, oats, and barley were grown and put through the thrasher to make straw. The straw was blown out and stacked with a hay fork. It supplied the bedding for the family. No complaining was tolerated, and there was little time to even contemplate slacking off because day-to-day survival was dependent on the cooperation of the entire family. The food needs for the family and the farm were immense and required hunting for birds and other small game.

Harold remembered his mom Annie as a tough woman who was no stranger to hard work. One day in the fall of 1927—an important season for corn harvesting—everyone was pulling ears of corn when Annie went into labor. She yelled for Edward around noon exclaiming, "My water has broken!"

Edward called out, "Naomi run to the house! Harold, get Doc!"

Then Edward lifted Annie in his arms and carried her into the house. Archie was born an hour later at 1:00 p.m., a full nine pounds and four ounces. Harold arrived with the doctor minutes before the birth, and both mother and son were healthy.

Edward walked out of the bedroom with the doctor and stopped. He looked at Harold and said, "God is great, isn't he?" Then, with a sigh, he said, "The corn is waiting. Let's get it all pulled. Naomi, stay here with your mom and meet your new baby brother."

The daily requirements on the farm prohibited any concept of maternity leave or well checkups. Everyone understood the importance of balancing workloads to meet the hunger needs of the family and livestock and gain capital for barter and trade. In other words, there was no rest for the weary and no excuse not to work. After all, work ensured survival.

The work needs on the farm affected school attendance. School began after Labor Day, and all grade levels were dismissed at noon to go home and work in the fields. The Depression eliminated schools' providing lunch, leaving the family as the source of nutrition. Schools stopped most non-essential activities and concentrated on the essential courses of reading, writing, and arithmetic. After a half day in school, Harold and his classmates harvested cornfields, shucked corn, and placed new seed in the corn crib. In addition, the sweet potatoes had to be turned up and gathered for the winter. The Frank family took particular care of sweet potatoes, which they used as a cash crop, keeping the best for sale.

After the two new houses were built in 1931, Edward used sawdust to insulate the older homes. For a small fee, he let neighbors use them to store their potatoes. He got the idea to use sawdust as insulation after learning that iceboxes were also insulated with sawdust that was placed between the thin galvanized metal and the outer frame. Using leftover framing, Edward lined a room in the old house using sawdust as the insulation and converted shelves into bins to hold the potatoes. The idea worked so well that some of the neighbors paid four dollars for

Cabin insulated with sawdust to store potatoes

each bin and stored their produce in Edward's insulated rooms, which was the goal Edward had in mind. During September and early October, Harold worked from noon until dark in the fields and returned home for supper. School resumed normal hours in October after the fall harvest.

If Edward required mechanical help, he relied upon Uncle Pharris (Robert Pharris Wood), who was Annie's brother and was also known as "RP." RP worked as a loom mechanic in a textile mill. During the 1930s the sparse textile mills in the area only opened for a few hours per week, but Pharris had developed a reputation as one of the best mechanics around and was promoted to the textile position of master fixer. RP's mechanical expertise was on display before the Great Depression when the Frank family got its first car—a Ford Model T. Uncle Pharris would often come over, first learning and then teaching the mechanical work to keep up the Ford. Harold always tried to accompany Pharris and learn anything mechanical. Sadly, for most of Harold's childhood and early teenage years there was little time to play, much less develop a social life.

The farm came first, and one of the most anticipated seasonal activities was hog-killing season, which was closely tied to the settlement patterns of the state. North Carolina had been settled by the English in the Coastal Plain, but the Piedmont, or old Backcountry and Mountains, were primarily Scotch-Irish and Palatinate Germans. Most were subsistence farmers and were poor to low middle class. The primary meat of the state was pork. Hogs were the perfect meat source due to their high reproduction rates and moderate upkeep. One hog yielded several hundred pounds of meat and kept families such as the Franks fed. Hog preparation, and, most importantly, barbecue, were common to all Tar Heel residents, and the cultural variations in barbecue are still a subject of pride and competition. However, much of the secret to the legendary pulled-pork and chopped barbecue in North Carolina is linked to the wood preference used in the smokehouse, as well as to the salt and red and black pepper used to season the hog quarters hanging in each smokehouse. The English settlements in the Coastal Plain kept a strict formula of regular vinegar and red and black pepper, but the Scotch-Irish and Germans of the Piedmont experimented with apple cider vinegar as well as tomatoes while maintaining the Eastern blend of red and black pepper. Interestingly, the regional differences produced are still argued about to this day. Edward, true to his cultural background, used apple cider vinegar to create the brine for the hog meat. Edward regimented all farm work into proper management, pushing resources to the limit. In animal husbandry, hog meat was his central concern.

The Franks slaughtered three large hogs per year and took care to save every part of the meat. The hogs were fed a mixture of grain and shelled corn but not the cobs because Edward stated, "There is no nutritional value in the cob." Most of the cobs were placed next to the outhouse for toiletry use along with the unused Sears catalogs. The family was instructed to keep some of the shelled corn separated and placed into one of the old houses. It was added to oats and barley and combined with some fish meal into a five-gallon slop bucket. This slop was mixed with table scraps and stirred together using an oak paddle. The hogs were fed this mix after supper each day. After the hogs were fattened up, Edward waited till the weather cooled and then the hog-killing season commenced.

In late November when the temperatures cooled to the point of the occasional hard frost, Edward sprang into action. Hog-killing preparation began. He sharpened four butcher knives and, with Harold's aid, brought out an eight-foot-long, three-foot-wide oak table and placed it near the smokehouse and beside the hog-scalding vat. He inspected and cleaned the empty meat hooks hanging in the smoke house. Everyone went to bed to get rest and, before daybreak, while it was cold, the hog killing started. Edward and Harold would be joined after breakfast by Uncles Pharris and Grady. In return for their help, Edward and Harold would assist Pharris and Grady's own hog slaughtering, continuing into late November and early December.

After breakfast the four walked to the hog pen where Edward, armed with the Remington single-shot .22 rifle, opened the pen to let the hogs come out. Edward looked at everyone and said, "Save everything but the squeal, and I'll shoot the hog so he doesn't squeal." The hogs were too large to run off as each one weighed five hundred pounds, so Edward walked up to the first and shot near head level with the barrel in the center of the hog's head just above the eyes. The hog fell over and Uncle Pharris stuck it with the sharpened butcher knife below the throat and cut to the heart before pulling the knife out and turning the hog to let the animal bleed out. While the blood was draining, the four went to the next hog and did the same until all three hogs were killed. Edward brought out the hog-scalding vat, a container large enough to hold each five-hundred-pound animal. A fire was built under the vat and water was poured into the vat until it was about halfway full. The water was heated to 150 degrees as measured by a thermometer. Over the years, Harold had learned that barely running a finger across the water three times before being burned also indicated that the water was 150 degrees. A hook was placed through the hog's jaw. The hook was connected by rope to a block and tackle. Usually Zeb was tasked with pulling the hog up and lowering it onto a utility trailer which was pulled to the hog vat. The men then slid each hog from the trailer into the hog vat using a chain, which gently lowered the hog into the vat. After a few minutes in the water, the hog was removed, the timing depending on when its hair began to come off. They placed the hog on oak boards level with the vat and picked and scraped away the remaining hair. After all the hair was removed, the rear legs of the hog were attached to hooks on a single tree and raised, with the hog's head hanging down. The men then gutted the hog, removing its internal organs.

Edward used an ax to cut down each side of the backbone. Cutting out the tenderloin, he removed the ribs with a small ax. Starting at the base of the back, the head was cut off and carefully butchered. The side meat (midlands) of the hog was cut off to use for bacon. Afterwards, the hams and shoulders were removed. The backbone was laid on the table and chopped apart by ax, and the meat was removed from the bones. The two hams, the two shoulders and the two midlands were laid on the table and trimmed. Then the process started again with the next hog. The meat was placed on shelves in the smokehouse overnight.

The next day the six hams, shoulders, and midlands were rubbed in salt and placed inside the meat box, which had an inch of salt on the bottom, and the lid was closed. After five weeks, the meat was removed, and the excess salt was washed off and then peppered with a mix of black and red pepper. Burlap feed sacks were used to place the meat leg pointing down, and a piece of cardboard was placed between the leg bone and sack to keep it from getting too greasy. This prevented flies from getting to the meat and prevented worms from forming within. The sacks were tied and hung on hooks with the leg pointing down. The other meat, including the shoulders and midlands, was hung similarly.

The trimmed meat from the hams, shoulders, and midlands was seasoned with sage, red and black pepper, and salt. Sections of fat commonly called "fatback" were cut into squares then thrown into the washpot, which was outside sitting on three bricks over a fire. The fatback was cooked and stirred with a four-foot-long oak paddle that enabled its user to keep his distance from the danger of severe burns. Edward was vigilant in ensuring that kids and others stayed away from the cooking lard, which would cause serious burns. The lard press had a pot through which liquid fat was pressed by a plate at the top of the press that squeezed the grease out of the cracklings. The liquid grease flowed out of the spout into a lard can that could hold fifty pounds of lard. Then the lard press and hand grinder were used to make the sausage and lard. The pressed fat that survived the lard press was considered "rendered," leaving small crisp pieces called "crack-lings" that were placed in another can to be saved for use in making a delicious pan of "cracklin' cornbread." The remaining grease was gathered and cooked with unused parts of the hog that would still create grease. That grease would be used for lye soap made after the hogs were processed. Annie and Naomi washed and cleaned the small intestines wrong side out and took them to Edward and Harold who used them in sausage making. The sausages were made several feet long and hung over poles in the smoke house. A fire was built on the dirt floor with oak and hickory hardwoods, and then green brush such as cedar was used to make smoke. The smoking lasted an hour or more before Edward and Harold would enter to remove the ashes and close up the smokehouse. After working two days, the exhausted men came in to finally clean up and rest. The next morning they cleaned all of the equipment and tables. Edward and Harold prepared to help Grady and Pharris with their hog killing.

In the aftermath of the hog killing Annie made lye soap. She cooked it in a ten-gallon washpot with a mixture of the hog fat from the unusable parts of the head, the gut fat, and the grease from the cracklings that didn't go into the sausage but would still make grease. The fat was placed in the washpot over a fire. Water, ashes from the wood cookstove, and, on later occasions, Red Devil lye powder, finished the ingredients. The contents were cooked to the point where most of the water evaporated. Afterwards the fire was extinguished, and the contents of the pot were cooled into a solid. This was removed and cut into pieces of soap. The soap was used for personal hygiene and for cleaning clothes and bedsheets. The resourcefulness was true to Edward's word: "Save everything but the squeal, and I'll shoot the hog so he doesn't squeal."

During the hog season of 1935, another neighboring farm still had to slaughter hogs, so Harold walked over to see if they needed his help. The Jones family was all too happy to receive his it. Harold noticed the Joneses were behind, so he helped bring out the oak butchering table and checked the smokehouse. Mr. Jones told his son to bring out the rifle to shoot the hog that Harold had just turned out. The young boy fired and shot the hog between the eyes. The hog squealed but did not die. Mr. Jones yelled and said, "Let Harold shoot the hog!" Harold grabbed the rifle and noticed the boy used .22 shorts instead of .22 long rifle bullets. Harold felt in his pocket, found a .22 long rifle bullet, and changed out the round. He then shot the hog in the right spot. The hog fell dead.

Mr. Jones yelled, "That's how you kill a hog. Let Harold show you how. He knows what he is doing!"

"Yes, sir," said the boy as Harold bled out the hog.

CHAPTER 3

The Art of Turtle Meat

When Harold was six, Edward began his survival training—starting with the slingshot that he carried most of his young life. Edward taught him to construct the slingshot using a dogwood tree. A limb that had a strong fork an inch or two thick and was malleable enough to pull together while still green worked great. After locating the perfect limb, he created a tailor-made slingshot. To construct it, Harold peeled off the bark and bent the fork to his personal preference. He then fixed the tines in place using metal bailing wire. Harold carefully cut grooves with his pocketknife to attach the sling. He laid the fork on an oven rack and baked it at approximately 350 degrees until it turned brown. He removed the cured fork and, after it cooled, removed the bailing wire. The final step was to attach the rubber sling and leather tongue to complete the weapon. Harold had perfected his slingshot making skills by the age of eight.

The slingshot making talent was a family trait. Harold's sister Naomi could make a slingshot as well as anyone. More importantly, she could use a slingshot or gun to garner small game. Harold and Archie searched for additional food during the Great Depression with a flashlight or the help of a clear, moonlit night by hunting birds nesting in or near the haystacks. Black birds, sparrows, and occasional woodpeckers would nest in the hay and become sustenance for the Franks. Harold learned that the tastiest were robins, meadow larks, and black birds, but even woodpeckers would do. After picking off birds with the slingshot, Harold would field dress each bird and carry them on a stick to the family fireplace where the birds were cooked and consumed. There were many times when Harold brought home enough for his mom to stew. This resourceful attitude taught Harold to craft deadly slingshots that he put to great use hunting birds and small game. He did anything to help ease the hunger pangs common during the Great Depression. The thought of becoming dependent upon others or the government was unthinkable. The family, church, and community combined to create a foundation of mutual support. Receiving help came with no disrespect as long as the individual receiving the help displayed one admirable trait: a willingness to work without complaint or excuse.

Other than the pork, Edward loved turtle meat the most, and he reminded the family on several occasions that, "One good-size mud turtle could provide several meals." Edward's routine to catch and prepare the turtle for the wood cookstove became a product of artwork. Harold often accompanied Edward to the creek banks of Swearing, Abbots, and Dutchman's Creeks where they would seine and gravel for turtle and catfish. This was not a fun-and-games adventure for father-and-son bonding, but a quest for food to ensure the family wouldn't starve. Edward graveled under the creek bank and would feel under the water until he located a mud turtle. After finding its head, Edward grabbed him by the neck and near the tail, rendering the turtle immobile. He walked toward a sand bar where he always kept a freshly cut stick, commonly called a "green stick." He would kill the turtle with the stick by striking a mortal blow on the nose of the turtle. Then he quickly returned to the creek to continue the quest for more mud turtles and catfish.

At home, Edward and Harold scalded the turtle in a number two wash pan the size of a foot tub. They brought the temperature to 150 degrees, a temperature that, as with hog killing, they could identify by running a finger through the water three times without burning. Then they placed the turtle, shell and all, in the pot to soak for a few minutes. When they removed the turtle, they flipped it upside down and cut apart the under shell from the meat and legs. They cut the meat off the top shell and cut the legs and neck off while being careful to keep the pieces of meat separated. To a mud turtle aficionado, each part of the turtle meat has a very distinctive taste and must be prepared correctly. They washed the meat, placed it in a pan, and salted it to be ready either for immediate cooking or to be placed in the icebox for future meals. Annie preferred to boil the meat. Some meat was rolled in flour and corn meal and deep fried in hog lard. In most cases the turtle meat meal was complimented with roasted ears of corn and Annie's homemade biscuits, which were used to gather up any sauce remaining on the plate because nothing was ever wasted. Many days during the 1930s, mud turtle, opossum, and wild birds provided the only meat that kept starvation at bay.

CHAPTER 4

Hard Times in the Cotton Patch: Christmas 1935

The Franks were devout Protestant Christians and lifelong members of Saint Luke's Lutheran Church in Tyro, North Carolina, roughly three miles from their farm. Harold could recite the Apostle's Creed as a teenager and, true to his Protestant beliefs, he carefully repeated, "Holy Christian Church" so as not to make the mistake of saying, "Holy Catholic Church." John 3:16 was Harold's favorite Bible verse, and it stayed with him throughout the darkest times during World War II: "For God so loved the world, that he gave his only begotten Son, that whosoever believeth in him should not perish, but have everlasting life." The independence of his Protestant upbringing taught respect and a personal relationship with Christ that no priest or bishop could come between. Annie and Edward believed in treating people fairly and giving everyone a chance, just as Christ would. They instructed their children to keep

PFC Frank's Bible dedication page from Annie, May 3, 1943

their word and finish what they started. Seldom did the Frank family miss a church service. The mere thought of deliberately missing a service, even because of exhaustion, was as sinful as missing work.

In 1935 Naomi, being the oldest at thirteen years, and just two years older than Harold, decided to find a way to help their parents through the misery of the Depression. On Friday, October 18, 1935, Naomi looked at Harold as they were finishing picking cotton on their farm and said, "Harold bring your sacks of cotton over here with mine. I've got an idea." Harold went to her, and they counted each other's sacks of cotton.

"How'd you do that?" Harold asked. "You beat me by one sack again!"

Naomi laughed and then looked serious, "Harold we need to help Dad and Mom. I've got an idea." Harold looked up, and Naomi continued, "Let's go over to the Frittses' farm and pick cotton and pool our money together to buy Dad and Mom something special for Christmas." Harold agreed.

That evening at supper Naomi looked at Annie and Edward and said, "Harold and I want to pick a little more cotton at the Frittses' farm."

Edward looked at Annie and back at Naomi and then finally at Harold and said, "Harold you've worked hard this week and we're caught up. It's up to you. If you two want some extra work, go ahead."

The next morning the two walked to the Frittses' farm.

Bob Fritts was the owner and was one of the best cotton farmers in the county. His farm bordered the Franks' farm, and his farmhouse was less than a mile away. He grew "Texas Big Bowl" long-strand cotton. Cotton picking did not start until after the morning dew had dried up, which usually meant the cotton was dry around 9:00 a.m. Naomi and Harold arrived at the Frittses' place and knocked on the door. The Frittses' young daughter, Zula Fritts, answered the door and said, "Hey, Naomi and Harold."

"We are looking for Mr. Bob to pick some cotton," Naomi replied. Most of the neighbors commonly referred to Mr. Fritts as Mr. Bob.

Zula said, "We've had a good crop as you can see, and Dad said we needed some help. He's in the barn right now."

"Thanks, we'll go find him," Naomi said.

At the barn, Mr. Fritts was feeding his horses and saw Naomi and Harold, so he stopped to speak with the Frank youngsters.

"Mr. Bob," started Naomi and Harold, "we would like to pick some of your cotton. We're hoping to make some extra money for Edward and Annie."

"That's okay with me," Mr. Fritts said. "I trust you two." Looking down the road to one of the nearby tenant farms, Mr. Fritts sighed and turned back, "You two are one of the few that won't put rocks in the sacks. I've always trusted your family." Rubbing his hand quickly across Harold's hair he pointed and said, "There are sacks already by the edge of the cotton field, and I'll bring y'all some more. How long will you two work?"

"Till dark," Harold and Naomi said together.

Looking somewhat surprised, Mr. Fritts replied, "Okay, then go ahead, and I'll weigh the sacks when y'all finish."

Harold and Naomi worked, taking only a short lunch break when they ate the cured ham and baked sweet potatoes they had brought with them. By dark Naomi had six sacks of cotton, about three hundred pounds. Harold was working on his fifth sack, and Naomi came over and helped him finish. The two rested and Mr. Fritts came over with a horse team and stopped to look at the sacks. "Y'all did pretty good," he said. "Let's get the sacks on the wagon and weigh them up." As Naomi guessed,

Mr. Fritts weighed six hundred pounds of cotton, which brought them three dollars. These were Depression wages, and they totalled out to about eighteen cents an hour for eight hours of back-breaking, grueling work.

After being paid, Naomi and Harold said, "Thank you, Mr. Bob," and they all shook hands.

"Thank you," replied Mr. Fritts, "and come back whenever you need to. See you two at church in the morning."

On December 14, 1935, Edward loaded the family in the Model T and traveled to downtown Lexington, North Carolina, to do their Christmas shopping. The family separated, going to different stores. Harold went to McCulloch's Dime Store and bought Edward a new pair of socks for twenty-five cents and a pack of pocket handkerchiefs for another twenty-five cents. The dime stores had recently popped up across the nation, some becoming giants like Woolworth. Harold favored McCulloch's, a local, family-owned store that had people he knew working there. Harold looked at sewing equipment that Annie could use for her Singer sewing machine, and he found a package containing needles, thread, and a thimble. He had enough change left over to buy some candy corn and a mix of fudge and candy. At a different dime store, Naomi purchased a pack of handkerchiefs and some hosiery for Annie and a pair of nice, sturdy work gloves for Edward. After returning home Naomi wrapped the presents she and Harold had bought for their parents to go under the Christmas tree.

Tuesday, December 24, was Christmas Eve, and the family woke with excitement. Chores had to be completed earlier than usual in order to have time to decorate the tree and the house for Christmas. After dinner Edward looked at Harold and said, "You ready to get the tree?"

"Yes, sir. You want that cedar we looked at Saturday?" asked Harold.

Edward smiled and, glancing at Annie, said, "Son, let's go." The two went to the barn, hitched Nellie and Gray to the wagon, and left to locate the right cedar tree in the lower pasture. They brought the tree to the house. Edward nailed it to a cross plank and stood it up in the front room. That evening the family decorated the tree with color paper strands and a few strings of popcorn. Naomi and Harold put their presents under the tree before going to bed, and Edward and Annie placed more presents later that evening.

Before breakfast on Christmas Day, the family gathered at the tree and exchanged presents. Harold, Naomi, and Archie each got a shoe box filled with brazil nuts, pecans, hard candy, an apple, and an orange. Harold was surprised when he opened a present to find a twenty-five-cent dump truck with a D-size battery that turned on the truck's headlights. This was the best gift ever, yet Edward warned, "Harold, you're in charge, but let Archie use it some. But when the battery runs down, that's it." So Harold and Archie would turn on the lights briefly before they removed the battery to conserve its life.

Annie looked at her presents, stared at Naomi and Harold with her eyes watering, and said, "You two should have bought something for yourselves."

Harold quickly interrupted and said, "Nah, Momma, we wanted to get you something." Then Harold walked over to Annie and gave her a hug.

With her arm around Harold's shoulder and her eyes turned toward Naomi, Annie smiled while stating, "You two worked hard and could've found something you needed."

Naomi hugged Edward and said, "We know things are hard, but Harold and I picked cotton at the Fritts place to try to help. Merry Christmas, Momma and Daddy!"

Annie looked at Edward, and both held hands while smiling at their children and telling them, "Merry Christmas." Annie stood up and walked by the Christmas tree and began to sing "Silent Night" with her alto voice. Everyone joined in and—at least for one day—took a bite off the Great Depression.

The Depression, family values, and Christian faith taught the Franks frugality, responsibility, and honorable living. They took care of everything they had, which wasn't much. What they did have they appreciated and kept in good working order. This same attitude carried the family through wherever they went. Harold remembered the power going out once during a fall revival service. The power loss caused the sanctuary to go dark, but the preacher continued preaching. Archie had developed a reputation for fixing electrical issues, and without hesitation he took the initiative to seek out the problem. Meanwhile the preacher continued, and when he was nearly finished delivering the gospel, the lights suddenly came back on. Archie quickly returned to his seat next to Harold. Edward smiled, walked up to the revival preacher, and said "Preacher, you didn't read that sermon from a paper. You must be a pretty good preacher." He then turned to Archie and patted him on the shoulder. Religion, hard work, and "waste not, want not" thriftiness described the Frank existence during the Depression.

CHAPTER 5

Hunting with Uncle Pharris

L earning to shoot was second nature to Harold Frank, especially in a society where missing game on the first shot meant your shirttail being cut. Clothing was expensive, and no one wanted to lose a shirttail over a careless shot. Therefore, understanding how the weapon operated became second nature, and the conservation of costly ammunition was a major concern. Edward gave Harold a Daisy BB gun on his sixth birthday. He could only shoot at targets from which the used BBs could be easily retrieved—from a soft wooden box that had once held 12-gauge shotgun shells, for instance. After proving proficiency with a BB gun, Harold graduated to a 12-gauge shotgun that Edward taught Harold to shoot by targeting objects in trees. Objects were tossed in the air to teach Harold the art of "wing and shot" necessary for quail hunting—which was more commonly called "Bobwhite hunting." In the Frank family, as was common throughout the region, gun skill was as crucial as planting corn. The Great Depression placed considerable weight upon hunting small game, as well as the yearly hog killing, to keep the family fed with meat.

Uncle Pharris, like most of their farming neighbors, had an English Pointer hunting dog. Other relatives had setters. All were trained to hold to "wing and shot," meaning, the bird dog would locate a covey of quail and point immediately. The quail, sensing the situation, would hold tight and motionless until the pointer or hunter moved close. The hunter hoped that the bird dog would remain on point until the hunter caused the covey to flush and take to its wings. The birds could then be shot. If the shot were successful, the dog would break the point and retrieve the bird. That is the meaning of "wing and shot." The immediate concern would be that of the pointer jumping the point before the hunter was ready or, worse, running after the bird while the hunter was shooting. The inherent danger was injuring another hunter or a dog. Safety was a vital concern. To be a good bird hunter meant being resourceful. One had to understand the weapon being carried, the ability of those hunting, and the behavior and ability of the bird dog. Understandably, the hunting dog was considered a part of the family.

Uncle Pharris had an eight-cylinder Buick Roadster. He would whistle and his pointer would jump up and lie between the fender and radiator, where nothing was able to knock the dog off. When they arrived at a field and parked, the pointer would wait until Uncle Pharris got out and walked to the front of the car. This was the signal for the pointer to dart off into the field while Harold and Pharris waited for him to point. No one could remove the dog from the fender otherwise. He was truly RP's loyal companion. RP's pointer was a hunter and a wonder one had to see to believe. By the time RP had trained the animal, no whistle or voice command was needed. RP would walk to the front of the car with his shotgun and motion for the dog. Quickly the pointer sprang from the Roadster and rushed off into the field. RP told everyone, "Just remain still until he points."

The challenge in quail hunting was working together to gain the meat without injury to man or dog. Edward and Uncle Pharris cautioned, "Know the equipment, understand the game, and aim small, miss small." Once a covey of birds was flushed, they hunted the singles, and Pharris stated, "Never let a covey get below five birds because at that number the covey is susceptible to other prey and may not produce enough for the following year." As they began each hunt, Pharris would laugh and say with a smile, "Shoot well 'cause I'm not giving you any that I bring down."

After Harold mastered the shotgun, Edward introduced him to the rifle. Harold began with a single-shot .22 caliber Remington rifle. Harold was never allowed to waste a single round, and when hunting, Edward told Harold, "Listen to me son: if you kill it, you skin it." Harold became intimately familiar with each weapon in the Frank arsenal and could assemble and disassemble each before he reached eleven years of age. In 1936 on his twelfth birthday, Edward looked at Harold, motioned to Uncle Pharris and said, "I know the best present for you, son. You can pick whatever gun you need, and from now on you will be hunting with Uncle Pharris. You'll learn all there is to know about hunting, guns, and cleaning game." Harold was overjoyed at the chance to learn from the expert, RP.

Uncle Pharris taught Harold everything he knew about tracking, catching, and killing game. Before each hunt for the Southern Bobwhite, Pharris reminded Harold, "Don't rush or waste a shot. Try to get two birds with one shot. Once they flush, let the pointer do the work. Never run after him or follow him as he hunts. Just be still and have patience." Looking over the farms, Uncle Pharris put his hand on Harold's shoulder and said, "We've got too much else to do. It's time for the dogs to work. Wait for him to point, then walk to the dog and look in front of its nose a few feet and move up. You go left, and I'll go right." The pointers would point and, once the bird was hit, retrieve the bird and return to hunting across the farmland. Meanwhile, Harold and RP would wait for the next point.

On his first quail hunting trip, Harold quickly learned to remain steady as the covey flushed and to shoot only when two quail crossed each other, thus getting two birds with one shot. There was no need to rush the shot because the pointer would find the singles. Cooperating as a team and understanding the habits of an English pointer trained Harold to have patience. He was taught to lead the shot for birds moving left or right, and he became proficient all around at wing and shot. He also learned

to conserve ammunition. In addition, just as Harold had learned
to care for each horse, he learned to recognize when the dogs
needed water or, more commonly, needed briars or other thorns
removed from the pads of each paw. Harold and Uncle Pharris
would bird hunt during the day and "coon" (raccoon) hunt at
night. Harold learned to disassemble, clean, and fix the rifles
and shotguns. Pharris instructed Harold: "Before you ever shoot
a gun, know how it works. If you take care of it, it will take care
of you. And always keep the barrel clean." Pharris looked at
Harold and warned him, "Your Iver Johnson 12 gauge fires these
paper cartridges at six hundred to eight hundred pounds per
square inch, so don't let that barrel get dirty. You can put away
that slingshot. You won't be needing it for a while."

Opossum hunting was a joint endeavor and one of Edward's
favorites. No one questioned Edward on the art of opossum or
turtle hunting. He was considered the expert. Edward used his
own black and tan hounds named Rock and Riley. These dogs
treed both opossums and raccoons. Edward, Pharris, and
Harold would locate tracks, which were most commonly found
near creek banks. Then Edward would release the dogs from
their leads, and the men would stand patiently. They waited for
the sounds of eager hounds baying at opossums they had forced
up a tree. Once the prey was treed, all went to locate the spot
and shine a light to locate the cornered animal. Uncle Pharris
and Harold would do the tree climbing to capture the opossum
alive. Once several had been caught, they would call it a night
and head back to the farm. The dogs were fed and watered, and

then the captured prey was placed into a pen where it was fed persimmons for several days to ease the gaminess of the meat. The goal was to capture six to eight opossums. Edward and Uncle Pharris thought opossum meat second to a mud turtle. They taught Harold proper opossum skinning, which, done correctly, brought a feast that Uncle Pharris never missed.

Using a pocketknife he slit the throat by first picking up the opossum by its tail and using the other hand to grab the animal by the back of the its neck. He then released the tail and freed the first hand to stab the opossum in the neck for the kill, and then drained the blood. Then he dipped the opossum in a bucket of cold water until fully immersed. After removing it, he dipped the animal into another pot of hot scalding water. The fur came off almost immediately, and a hatchet was used to chop off the nose area just below the eyes, followed by the feet and tail. Afterwards the opossum was gutted and barbecued over an open pit of hot coals while Annie Frank placed sweet potatoes on the fire for two to three hours to slow-roast them. Once the meat was pulled from the barbecue pit, it was added to Annie's buttermilk biscuits, which were made with lard and freshly-churned butter. Opossum meat, like mud turtle meat, helped ease the hunger pangs of the Great Depression.

In the process of hunting with Uncle Pharris, Harold found that his favorite wild animals were rabbits. This small game was bountiful and much easier to prepare than turtle. Harold would come home and show his brother Archie how to set rabbit traps. They mostly used box traps, but there were other methods. A particular favorite was a two-foot-long hollow log. The trap didn't require much for bait but the occasional piece of apple. When a rabbit was caught, Harold used the same technique he knew from opossum hunting. To skin the rabbit, he would grab it with his pocketknife, stick the rabbit through the throat to the heart, and let it bleed out. He next cut around its tail and pull the fur to its head. Then he removed the hide and gutted the rabbit of organs, keeping only the liver. The cleaning process, especially the removal of the hide, was much quicker than an opossum—but, at least according to the Frank family, the final product was not as tasty.

Annie boiled rabbit in a way that was very similar to the method she used for mud turtles. Once tenderized, the rabbit meat was rolled in flour and cornmeal for frying. The sides served with rabbit were different than with turtle. Annie would cook beans canned during the summer and add mashed potatoes. Then she baked cornbread from the wood cookstove.

During Harold's youth, Uncle Pharris became as close to Harold as any best friend or school teammate. The knowledge, lessons, and experiences he taught Harold were an important part of the young man's upbringing. Harold had no idea that all this knowledge and experience would soon become vital for keeping himself and several U.S. Army soldiers alive in World War II.

By 1939 under the guidance of Edward and Uncle Pharris, Harold had mastered every part of farm life from hitching horse teams, slaughtering hogs, and milking cows to the maintenance of the old McCormick-Deering tractor, the Model T, and the sawmill. Harold could repair farm equipment, he was a master gunsmith, and he had become an expert hunter. For most of the families growing up during the Great Depression, Harold's life and knowledge were nothing unusual. Life was hard, so boys and girls were expected to be adults early. Excuses and complaining weren't tolerated, and work wasn't finished until a task was entirely completed. Pain was meant to be endured and treated later when time allowed. However, in the Bible Belt, despite the hard work, there was no excuse for missing church on Sunday morning. Furthermore, despite the labor and the constant hunger during the week, the thought of hunting on Sunday was unacceptable. On a fall hunting trip in 1939, Harold and Uncle Pharris walked into the house. Harold greeted Edward not by the usual "Dad" or "Sir" but, "Hello Pap," which brought a smile to Edwards's face—and thereafter a new name.

CHAPTER 6

Faith, Sports, Walter Winchell, and That Damn T-Model

B eginning in the summer of 1939, the Great Depression eased enough so that the Frank extended family met on a rotational basis at different homes. These family reunions brought at least one hundred relatives. Each family arrived with a covered dish, which usually consisted of fried chicken, country ham, corn bread, green beans, and biscuits. Edward was good at making arrangements to ensure all had plenty to eat. Every year brought another exciting Frank Family Homecoming. On the Fourth of July of both 1939 and 1940, Harold, Edward, Uncle Grady, and other relatives went to Dutchman's Creek in Davie County. They seined the creek in deep water and pulled out catfish, brim, a few bass, and sometimes Pap's favorite, a mud turtle. The goal was to catch enough fish to provide plenty of meat for the Frank family reunion. The men cleaned the catch on the banks. Then they took the catch to the women, who would fry the fish rolled in cornmeal while corn bread cooked in a cast-iron skillet. They had fish, chicken, and country ham from the various farms, plus dessert consisting of cakes and pies. Food was plentiful for all. These reunions were remembered as the Depression version of the "Feeding of the Five Thousand" from biblical times. After eating, the family sat around and talked about the Depression, family, farming, and world concerns while Harold, Archie, and the other cousins went swimming.

After the celebration on July 4, 1940, Harold and Glenn decided to escape the summer heat and go down to the swimming hole in the creek next to farmer Joe Sink's place. Harold and Glenn splashed and jumped off the banks, challenging each other to make the biggest splash before walking up the creek toward another swimming hole. A fence line just above the water stopped the boys. Harold yelled, "Glenn, I'll hold the wire and you go under." Harold grabbed the line and instantly felt an electric shock which threw him back into the knee-deep water and caused him to yelp in pain. When he got up, he saw Glenn looking stunned.

"I've never seen an electric fence before," Glenn said.

"Well, whatever you do, don't touch this one," replied Harold, as he shook and stared in disbelief at his hand. It still tingled from the shock.

The world the Franks lived in was separated by religious views in a denominational manner. As in most Southern towns and rural farmlands, the Baptists abstained from the consumption of alcohol for the most part. This had not always been the case, but during the Great Temperance Revivals of the 1830s, most of the Baptists and some Methodists turned away from drinking alcohol. The Baptists also decreed that dancing posed a dangerous threat to one's soul when combined with alcohol. According to early Baptist ministers, evil and social disruption awaited those who indulged. As a result, a new Southern beverage swept the South. It was called, "Baptist beer," or more commonly, "sweet tea." In New Bern, North Carolina, Pepsi-Cola emerged to supply carbonated soft drinks to the Carolinas. Coca-Cola did the same in Atlanta, Georgia. The market for non-alcoholic soft drink beverages swept the Bible Belt. It wasn't long before other North Carolina soft-drink companies emerged, such as Royal Crown (RC) and Cheerwine. They were eager to supply the growing Baptist and related denominational members with alcohol-free drinks. The hard drinks, commonly called "moonshine" or "white lightning," were derived from corn and distilled to release a dangerous concoction of 160-proof whiskey. But for now, it was kept out of sight. Other enterprising individuals used apples to create "applejack," or peaches to make a brandy. Even though the South appeared to have gone off spirits, wine, and beer cold turkey, many in the region became quite skilled at chemistry. Their products were just kept behind the barn and away from the preacher.

The Frank family made their first sweet tea with ice in 1939. The ice came from the block of ice in the icebox and was chipped by using a small, handheld ice pick. The money to buy the tea bags only gave them tea to drink for Sunday dinner. Harold didn't get to experience soft drinks until May of 1940. Edward and Harold sold some of their strawberries out of the T-Model Ford in downtown Lexington. They made enough money to go to Stamey's Barbeque stand where they bought a hot dog and Coca-Cola for ten cents.

The Franks were Lutheran, which made them theologically distinct in an important way from their Baptist brethren: alcohol in moderation was acceptable. Edward and Annie made wine, which they tended to as carefully as any of the other work requirements on the farm. The new homes that Edward, Uncle Grady, and Harold had built had a basement cellar where they kept three large twenty-gallon stone crocks. The Franks had reputedly one of the best-soiled strawberry patches in the area and also did quite well with both their muscadine and Concord grapevines. Annie made jelly from some of the delicious fruit, but most of the grapes were dedicated to the three crocks, seeds and all. The fermentation of the fruit was observed daily. When a skim formed, Annie and Edward would remove it. After several days they strained the contents to capture the juice. They poured the contents carefully into jugs or bottles. The tops were left open, because if they capped the bottles while the fermented nectar was still bubbling up, the jugs or bottles would crack. When bubbles subsided, they capped the jugs. The process took three weeks to a month. The yearly goal was about ten gallons of wine.

The Franks never sold the wine but instead gave a few bottles to people who helped them around the farm with major events, like harvesting wheat or putting up straw with the hayfork. This got the attention of the Lutheran congregation. Unlike the Baptists, the Lutheran denomination remained loyal to the Catholic tradition of using wine for communion. The Baptists themselves had remained loyal to the grape until the temperance revivals, which led to their preachers adopting wine's first cousin for use in church—grape juice. The Great Depression significantly affected the tithes and offerings of all the denominations, including the congregation at St. Luke's Lutheran Church, which couldn't afford to buy communion wine. Here, and on other special occasions, the congregation turned to the Frank family vintage. Edward would arrive at the church on communion days with the "Frank" vintage, and all became cleansed by the blood of the Cross.

When Harold started high school the "communion sip" was replaced with a glass of wine. After particularly long days of chores and farming, Harold would come in the house, and Annie would pour Harold a glass of wine to sip while warming up in front of the fireplace. This was a very special event, as Harold and Naomi were accustomed to only Annie and Edward drinking a glass of wine, and then only two or three times per week. Edward discussed the dangers of alcohol and warned that some people could not handle drinking. He stressed moderation. At one point, Edward looked at Harold one evening and warned, "Some people can't just drink a glass of wine or whiskey." While shaking his head, he frowned and stated to Annie, "They won't stop till it's gone and will spend money needed for their family, or farm, to buy more." Then looking back at Harold, he asked, "Do you understand, son?"

"Yes, sir," replied Harold.

After turning fourteen in 1938, Harold was considered to be a young adult and was expected to do almost anything Edward could do around the farm. The most important achievement still in store was to become saved. Harold went to Lutheran catechism school a few months before turning fourteen. The school lasted for two weeks until the student understood and memorized the Apostles' Creed. Harold's pastor, C. C. Pless, talked to the class of four students seeking divine intervention. About a week into the class, while listening to the theology of Christ, Harold felt the light bulb turn on in his heart and mind. Quickly, Harold both understood and memorized the Apostles' Creed. The following Sunday as the family prepared for church, Annie walked up to Harold, who was standing in the den. She looked at her son and said, "This is a special day. I'm proud of you son. So, don't be nervous. You know the Creed."

Harold replied, "I know, Momma. I'm ready. Naomi had me recite it to her all week long."

As Edward and Naomi walked toward the door, Naomi turned to Harold and said, "You're going to do a good job."

The family loaded into the 1927 Model T and drove to church. At church Pastor Pless introduced the new class of students and asked them to tell the congregation what they had

learned. Harold volunteered and stood up in front of the congregation. He looked at his mom, dad, and Naomi, then thanked
the pastor and said:

I believe in God, the Father almighty, maker of
heaven and earth,

And in Jesus Christ, his only Son, our Lord, who
was conceived by the Holy Spirit, born of the Virgin
Mary, suffered under Pontius Pilate, was crucified,
died and was buried. He descended into hell. The
third day he rose again from the dead. He ascended
into heaven and sits at the right hand of God the
Father Almighty. From there he will come to judge
the living and the dead.

I believe in the Holy Spirit, the holy Christian
Church, the communion of saints, the forgiveness of
sins, the resurrection of the body, and the life everlasting. Amen.

Once he completed the creed, Harold walked back to where
his four other classmates were seated. Afterwards, each got up
to do their own recitation. Pastor Pless then charged the congregation to always support each other and remember the power of
prayer. The students achieved the rite of Confirmation. As soon
as the service concluded, Edward placed his hands on Harold's
shoulders and said, "We're both proud of you." Harold felt he
had achieved the final qualification of manhood.

On Monday it was back to barn work. A close friend of
Edward, whom Harold only knew as Mr. Hedrick, was respected
for his ability to put up straw. He did it in such a way that the
outer layer would shed water, thereby keeping most of the stack
dry despite heavy rain. He was a man of legend as well. Earlier
in the threshing, Mr. Hedrick saved a neighbor's child who was
cleaning around the thresher machine and putting loose wheat
into the thresher. The child's arm became caught in the machine.
Mr. Hedrick immediately saw the danger. While the large belt
was running, he grabbed the belt with his hands and yanked it
off the pulley saving the boy's life, or at least the loss of a limb.
Somehow, Mr. Hedrick escaped any injury of his own. Not
surprisingly, his work and company were highly valued by
Edward. Each year after the grain had been threshed and the
straw stacked, Edward would reward him with a bottle of the
Frank vintage wine. The wine was poured into a clean Coke
bottle and capped as a Coke bottle. Edward had acquired a
hand-bottling capper and would frequent the local Coca-Cola
bottling company and pick up unused caps. Threshing wheat
and stacking straw were worth every drop. The year he saved
the boy's life Mr. Hendrick received two bottles of the Frank
vintage.

Following the hay stacking, Edward's cousins Forrest and
Homer Penniger came to the farm. Harold received his work
clothes from Homer, who was two years older than Harold.
Forrest was himself older than Homer, and both were city boys
from Main Street, Lexington. Harold heard them laughing by

the barn and ran over to see what the two had gotten into. As Harold got close, he watched as each climbed on the straw stacks and promptly slid down the carefully arranged straw stacks. Harold warned, "You're not to play in the hay!" Ignoring Harold, they continued and laughed even louder.

Edward, hearing the excitement, rushed over to the barn and witnessed the destruction. Full of anger, Edward yelled, "Get out of the hay now! You two go home!"

While the boys ran home, Edward grabbed Harold by one arm and pulled off his belt with the other. Before getting a few lashes of the belt, Harold looked at Edward and said, "I couldn't help it. They're older and bigger than I am."

As Harold received his punishment, Edward said, "Maybe so, but that is our straw, needed for the year, and not a playground. Next time you'll know what to do. Do you understand?"

"Yes, sir," he replied.

Edward paused and said, "Take a stick to 'em next time."

A few weeks later the boys returned and once again went to the barn to do some hay sliding. Harold heard the commotion and ran up to the barn. Looking around the barnyard, he located a sturdy tree limb and broke off the smaller branches. Now armed with a stout stick, he walked to the bottom of the hay and said, "The first one that slides down a haystack I will bust so hard you'll never do it again! I ain't getting another whipping!" Without flinching he stared and waited. Neither of the boys tried to slide, and both backed away from the hay. Harold looked at them and said, "Now go home." They left, shaking their heads.

Harold felt a new sense of courageous manliness come over him. He smiled and threw the stick away from the barn, then returned home with a little more spring in his step.

In the same way Edward warned Harold about too much alcohol, he also told him to avoid tobacco and prohibited Harold from smoking or chewing. "Some folks," Edward began, "smoke and can't ever stop, wasting both time and money. Do you understand me?"

Harold replied, "Yes, sir," knowing that getting caught with even a chew would invite a beating. Such was the Frank family doctrine. Things were a little different with Harold's close friend Glenn Norman.

When the days were hot, Glenn would join Harold to spend their rare free time swimming in one of the nearby creeks. Glenn had several younger brothers. They were named Fred, Wayne, and Dick. All of the Normans chewed Black Maria tobacco, but Harold refused to chew because of warnings from Pap. That changed one day after he turned sixteen. It was the summer of 1940. Harold had a day off from the farm and joined Glenn to go fishing along High Rock Lake. Glenn's dad, George, drove the boys to the lake. Against his better judgement, Harold accepted a chew of tobacco from Glenn. With no experience in the matter of chewing, Harold swallowed some of the tobacco juice as the two prepared to fish.

Glenn noticed that Harold had started sweating and became quiet. He considered and asked, "You all right?"

Harold, feeling nauseated, replied, "No, I'm not all right."

Glenn laughed, but with some concern. "Did you swallow the tobacco?"

"No, just some of the juice," Harold said.

"Oh my! You're going to be sick and dizzy," Glenn replied.

"I already feel it and can't go home like this because Pap will know, and I'll get a whipping."

Needless to say, he couldn't fish due to severe nausea. Finally, around midnight, still sick and too afraid to tell his dad, he returned home. George drove the boys back home and dropped Harold off along the way.

Harold approached the house from Uncle Grady's and was shocked to see Edward outside. Thinking trouble was coming, Harold slowed his steps. Pap looked up and saw Harold and yelled, "I need your help, son. We're trying to kill the wolf rats that are killing our chickens and dragging them underneath the outbuildings."

Harold yelled back, "Who is helping?"

"I am!" Archie said. "Come on before they get away!"

As Harold approached his dad, Edward asked, "Where's the fish?"

"I got sick and couldn't catch anything," Harold replied.

Edward looked at Harold with a strange expression and said, "Okay, I need you to help get up these rats!"

Harold, Archie, and their dad worked with the two black and tan hounds named Rock and Riley to find, locate, and kill the rats. The dogs successfully cornered the rats underneath two hog pens. Edward killed each rat when it ran out. It was a long night of rat killing and nauseating, tobacco stomachaches. Harold's quest for chew may have ended abruptly, but he was thankful that his secret never got out.

A week later the chance came to join the CCC (Civilian Conservation Corps) camp. Edward waited for Harold to finish his morning chores and then called out to his son to come over to Uncle Grady's. Harold arrived in time to hear the two men discussing a new water line that was being laid in at Uncle Grady's house. Edward and George Norman, Glenn's father, were to dig the ditch, but both looked at Harold and Glenn and handed them the pickaxe and shovel to do the digging. The boys were told to dig a trench two feet deep and one hundred fifty feet long. That depth was so the pipes wouldn't freeze in the winter. The summer heat was intense, but the two boys didn't complain to the adults. Harold and Glenn began whispering among themselves.

"When did this become a chore?" asked Glenn, who had the pickaxe.

"I don't know," Harold replied, "because yesterday I heard Pap say he and Uncle Grady were digging."

The two paused and wondered aloud, "Are we getting paid for this?"

Edward and Grady looked at each other and replied, "No!"

Feeling cheated, Harold whispered, "Tomorrow let's run off to the CCC camp where we'll get paid for this work."

"I'm game," Glenn said, "but we'll have to leave early before they get up."

Harold replied, "I heard that they pay twenty-five dollars per month, but you could only keep five dollars and the rest sent home."

"Any pay is better than nothing! It's forty miles from here to Pilot Mountain, but I'm ready to get paid."

The camps were products of FDR's New Deal, part of the plethora of projects remembered as the "alphabet agencies." The CCC was created to ease the Great Depression. Single men, often the second sons of families, left their homes, or in many cases farms, and arrived at federal camps complete with army-like barracks where they were placed on work teams. The teams cleared streams of debris and built roads and school-houses. In other cases they dug outhouses and took part in similar activities across the nation. The work done by the CCC and its cousin, the WPA (Works Progress Administration), was astounding. In North Carolina, the work achieved remarkable innovation with the construction of the Blue Ridge Parkway. Word carried and many left the farms to seek wages. The FDR administration faced a problem as few workers invested their wages, but hid them instead, mainly due to distrust in the banking system. The result was a continuance of the Great Depression because of little private industrial development. Harold and many others felt that FDR was at least trying to do something.

In North Carolina, Governor Gardner developed the Live at Home Plan. This plan included the development of the Agricultural Extension Agency, which came to one's hometown and employed farming experts, some of whom were from the state's agricultural school—NC State. They sought to help the family farm by teaching better land practices and, more importantly, by introducing pressure canning. The hope was to increase the survivability of family farms. As the old saying went, "Give a man a fish and he eats for a day. Teach him to fish and he will eat for a lifetime." The governor carried the philosophy over to food-storage methods, and the practice became a huge success. With some hard work and a small tract of dirt, almost anyone could grow enough corn, beans, and cabbage to sustain the family through the winter. Once again, the key was the willingness to work. The idea in some parts of North Carolina carried over to the churches. Church members would prepare a vacant or donated tract and work together to create "God's half acre." The produce went to feed local orphanages, the elderly, and others who had fallen on severe times.

As for Harold and Glenn, the two went to bed with a simple plan put together out of anger and born from busting red clay and shoveling out a ditch for no reward. It was carefully planned that before daylight each would grab some food and leave quietly. They would walk to the nearest CCC camp, which they knew to be somewhere near Pilot Mountain, North Carolina. Then they would finally enjoy the fruits of their labor and achieve monetary appreciation. Being extra careful not to upset Pap and Annie, Harold completed his chores and, after dark, made it to bed. Daylight came and went. Harold slept. So did Glenn. Two days later Glenn saw Harold and asked, "What happened? I thought you was coming over."

"I know, but I was too worn out," Harold replied.

Glenn laughed and said, "I figured. I overslept too."

As the summer of 1940 wore on, the Franks listened to the radio more frequently, particularly to Walter Winchell, Edward's favorite news reporter. The news occupied much of the conversation at the family gatherings. Hitler's rise to power and invasion of Poland, combined with Japan's threat to the Pacific, generated tension. Harold at the time was a sixteen-year-old basketball player at Tyro High School. His six-foot-two height helped push his team to conference championships. Playing sports became, in essence, another chore. Harold ran the three miles to the local basketball gym and played full games without resting on the bench. Afterwards he walked or ran the three miles back home to continue with his farm chores.

In the evening after the chores were completed, the family gathered around the radio at 7:00 p.m. and listened intently to Winchell. He began every broadcast with, "Good evening, Mr. and Mrs. America and all ships at sea." He went on to relay events from around the world. With each broadcast, Edward and Annie became more concerned that war was imminent. Harold's concerns still centered around chores, arriving on time for a game, or having hunting adventures with Uncle Pharris. If possible, Harold would tune into the radio on Wednesday at 5:00 p.m. to catch an episode of "The Lone Ranger." On Saturday night at 8:00 p.m., the family gathered around the radio to listen to the "Grand Ole Opry" broadcasting live from Nashville, Tennessee. They listened until bedtime at 9:30 p.m. Several times Harold overheard Edward say, "I wish I could go there just once."

The summer of 1940 was best remembered as the summer of the attack of the mud turtle. In July along Dutchman's Creek, Edward, Harold, and Glenn Norman were searching for mud turtles. On this particular trip to the creek, Glenn brought along his younger brother Dick, who was fifteen years old and deaf. Dick was deathly afraid of both turtles and snakes. Edward had disappeared beneath a creek bank, but soon emerged excited about finding a turtle. He dove quickly back into the water and pulled up a huge mud turtle. In the excitement of splashing through the water and rushing to the sand bar, where a green stick and sack awaited, he forgot about Dick's fear of turtles. Dick was seated, playing on the sand bar with his back to Edward. He turned around at the same time as he saw Edward rushing towards him with the giant turtle. Immediately Dick stood up. His eyes grew large as he stumbled backwards, falling into the water. He came up gasping for air and ran, falling several more times. During the commotion Harold and Glenn, both on their own mud turtle quest, turned and witnessed the scene. At first, they were confused as to what was happening, but as they watched it dawned on them. They laughed as Dick in desperation cleared the creek bank covered in mud and grass. Glenn and Harold yelled, "It's ok!" and ran towards Dick to calm him down. This only made him run farther and faster as he disappeared into the woods. Everyone realized what was going on except Dick who was in fear of his life and completely indifferent to the mud, briars, and tree branches he fled through. Laughing hysterically and almost out of breath, Harold finally caught up with Dick and wrestled him down. He motioned with his hands for Dick to calm down. Glenn finally caught up, and together they quieted the young man. Dick was not amused and wanted nothing more to do with the art of mud turtle hunting. Upon their return to the creek, Edward sat smiling at his accomplishment—and the meal awaiting him in the sack.

By the fall of 1940, the U.S. Army began expansion at several camps to prepare recruits for basic training. Edward had heard that contracts were being made for individuals with good construction experience to build new barracks. Edward applied for construction work at Fort Bragg, North Carolina. He received a contract in the spring of 1941. He left home and didn't return until that August. The Frank family had no telephone. Communication was confined to the U.S. Postal Service. On a Saturday in August, Edward drove into the yard with a brand new 1941 Chevy he had bought in Lexington for $913.

Sunday after a church service led by Pastor Pless, the Frank family returned home for Sunday dinner. Pap looked at everyone and said, "Do you know that our government has our boys running around with broomsticks instead of rifles for basic training?" Everyone look startled, and then Edward said to Harold, "Here's the key, I want you to take the Model T and go in the pasture and drive it until you know how to run it." All excited, Harold ate his dinner and then left for the pasture. Once Harold left, Edward informed Annie that events seem to indicate that war was on the way. Edward told Annie, "This will be another world war, and Harold would most likely have to fight because the Army will need everyone." The two continued to talk, and Edward expressed his worry that America needed industry to return and places to properly train the soldiers. Just as the two completed the parental discussion, which had lasted a full three hours, Harold returned with the Model T.

While his parents were still seated together in the living room, Harold ran in and yelled with excitement, "Pap, I figured it out!"

Edward and Annie looked up at Harold and smiled, and Edward said, "Good job, Harold." Annie gave him a hug and walked back into the kitchen. Edward stood and said, "Son, you'll be driving soon. There should be time later in the week for you to go and get a driver's license. Let's go back out and see you drive." The two left, and at the end of the week Harold went to the Lexington police station to take the license test.

A highway patrolman gave the verbal test, which Harold passed. He then looked at Harold. "Are you ready for the road test?" he asked.

"Yes, sir" replied Harold.

"Do you have a car?"

Harold pointed to the Model T and said, "Right over there."

"That damned old T-Model?" said the patrolman.

"Yes."

"Can you drive it?"

"Well, yes, I drove it up here."

"Come on back into the police station," the patrolman said. "You passed the driver's test."

Harold received his driver's license and was able to drive himself home. The only other person who was able to drive by himself to school at Tyro High School was Carson Swicegood, and that was only on special occasions.

Pap allowed Harold to drive sparingly as long as he paid the liability insurance to keep the farm out of jeopardy. Harold paid the insurance bill of thirty-six dollars per year. He earned the money by working at the Yadkin Finishing Company, a manufacturing facility that produced a bleacher for bed sheets and material for khaki uniforms. Harold took special care of the Model T. If he needed any mechanical advice, he got RP. The Depression era was still bleak, and it was hard work to survive, leaving little time for dating or other pleasures; but having a car did bring Harold more independence and responsibility.

December 7, 1941, began like most other Sundays. The Franks went to church and returned home for Sunday dinner. After finishing his meal, Harold asked to be excused. With a yes from his mom, he ran out the door to the Normans for a game of tag football. Typically, a game of football eventually led to baseball, which quickly ate up the afternoon. Tired from the game, Harold returned home to see the family listening to the radio. News bulletins came on declaring that the Japanese had destroyed much of the Pacific Naval Fleet at Pearl Harbor and caused considerable damage elsewhere on the Hawaiian Islands. The family was consumed with anger that such a thing had happened.

Uncles Grady and Pharris came over to discuss the war and the economy. Harold overheard many of their concerns. Edward told about the training at Fort Bragg with the substandard equipment and substitutes, such as broomsticks for rifles. He told Uncle Grady, "Our army is small and will need to fight on two fronts."

Pharris, being of a mechanical mind, stated, "We've got to have time to build the tanks, planes, and ships. With our naval losses, the West Coast could be attacked."

"If the Japs could do what they did at Pearl Harbor, they could attack California," Grady put in.

Edward said, "With England still holding on, I can't see Germany invading. But they will hit our ships."

Annie interrupted to remind them of President Roosevelt's Fireside Chat just before Harold's birthday in 1939. She said, "I don't agree with him on everything, but he told us to remember Christ."

FDR had stated:

> Some things we do know. Most of us in the United States believe in spiritual values. Most of us, regardless of what church we belong to, believe in the spirit of the New Testament—a great teaching which opposes itself to the use of force, of armed force, of marching armies and falling bombs. The overwhelming masses of our people seek peace—peace at home, and the kind of peace in other lands which will not jeopardize our peace at home.[1]

Annie said, "We all need to pray for those killed and wounded at Pearl Harbor."

"Amen to that," said Edward.

The next day, the Frank family joined many families across America to listen to FDR's address to the nation. Harold listened as well. All school classes had been canceled. Across the country people were fuming about and energized by the attack on Pearl Harbor. The nation gathered around radios to hear FDR's speech to Congress on December 8, 1941:

> Yesterday, December 7, 1941—a date which will live in infamy—the United States of America was suddenly and deliberately attacked by naval and air forces of the Empire of Japan.
>
> The United States was at peace with that Nation and, at the solicitation of Japan, was still in conversation with its Government and its Emperor looking toward the maintenance of peace in the Pacific. Indeed, one hour after Japanese air squadrons had commenced bombing in the America Island of Oahu, the Japanese Ambassador to the United States and his colleague delivered to our Secretary of State a formal reply to a recent American message. And while this reply stated that it seemed useless to continue the existing diplomatic negotiations, it contained no threat or hint of war or armed attack.

It will be recorded that the distance of Hawaii from Japan makes it obvious that the attack was deliberately planned many days or even weeks ago. During the intervening time the Japanese Government has deliberately sought to deceive the United States by false statements and expressions of hope for continued peace.

The attack yesterday on the Hawaiian Islands has caused severe damage to American naval and military forces. I regret to tell you that very many American lives have been lost. In addition, American ships have been reported torpedoed on the high seas between San Francisco and Honolulu.

Yesterday the Japanese Government also launched an attack against Malaya.

Last night Japanese forces attacked Hong Kong.

Last night Japanese forces attacked Guam.

Last night Japanese forces attacked the Philippine Islands.

Last night the Japanese attacked Wake Island.

And this morning the Japanese attacked Midway Island.

Japan has, therefore, undertaken a surprise offensive extending throughout the Pacific area. The facts of yesterday and today speak for themselves. The people of the United States have already formed their opinions and well understand the implications to the very life and safety of our Nation.

As commander in chief of the Army and Navy I have directed that all measures be taken for our defense.

But always will our whole Nation remember the character of the onslaught against us.

No matter how long it may take us to overcome this premeditated invasion, the American people in their righteous might will win through to absolute victory.

I believe that I interpret the will of the Congress and of the people when I assert that we will not only defend ourselves to the uttermost but will make it very certain that this form of treachery shall never again endanger us.

Hostilities exist. There is no blinking at the fact that our people, our territory, and our interests are in grave danger.

With confidence in our armed forces—with the unbounding determination of our people—we will gain the inevitable triumph—so help us God.

I ask that the Congress declare that since the unprovoked and dastardly attack by Japan on Sunday, December 7, 1941, a state of war has existed between the United States and the Japanese Empire.[2]

In school the next morning, the bombing and the speech were the main topics of conversation. Teachers and students alike believed without question that the United States was heading to war. All the students in Tyro High School were called into the auditorium for a special prayer. Every day, school began with a chapel service, but this time it would be longer. The principal, Roy Swicegood, stood on the small stage and told the students, "As you all know, our nation is now at war. I expect everyone to remain attentive and work to do the best you can. You can expect that many of you will find yourselves in military service. Let's all join together and pray." Harold, concerned for the future and thinking of the farm, couldn't remember the prayer.

Pearl Harbor had occurred during Harold's junior year, and the Great Depression was beginning to ease. Harold felt the war would end before he graduated the following year. Nevertheless, he knew that America was in a situation where war was inevitable with Japan in the Pacific and Germany across the Atlantic. The Frank family was still living a Depression lifestyle. Restarting a practically nonexistent industry to build the ships, tanks, guns, clothing, and barracks necessary to equip not thousands but millions of soldiers for combat needed to happen seemingly overnight. The nation geared up quickly.

Like many other Americans, Harold's ability to survive was about to be tested beyond comprehension. The war would be fought with one goal: to win at all costs and by all measures possible. Rationing became common. Industry had to turn from the production of normal products to that of armaments.

The rationing included food and fuel, and all manner of production began immediately. Millions volunteered and lined up at military recruitment stations. Others donated metal to be melted into military equipment. Across the nation factories feverishly opened to provide America the ability to fight a world war on two fronts. As history has recorded, the Greatest Generation, hardened by the Great Depression, with each citizen self-reliant, resourceful, oblivious to pain, without complaint, and—most importantly—unafraid of work in any condition, was getting ready to play its crucial role. The "Sleeping Giant" had awakened.

CHAPTER 7

Harold Is Drafted into the Army

In 1942, Harold Frank graduated from Tyro High School. High school only went to eleventh grade at the time, and Harold was one of sixteen who received their diplomas that year. The Frank family was one of the poorer in the class, but as Harold, smiling with pride, would state, "I had a car! Even if it was a Model T." As a seventeen-year-old with a diploma, Harold could work with minimum supervision in most machine shops, garages, sawmills, or farm equipment businesses, but for now he continued to work at the bleachery. Mr. Barnes, from the nearby township of Churchland, was Harold's supervisor. Both had known each other for years. To save on gas, Harold got permission to use the "family" bicycle, which technically was to be shared with his sister Naomi and younger brother Archie. Harold would bike three miles to Walser's Grocery Store, which was also a bus stop in Tyro. The bus went ten miles

Harold Frank's high school diploma

further, taking him to the finishing company. Harold used his wages to help the family farm and pay for gas to drive the Model T. He put aside extra funds from picking cotton on other farms to afford the insurance and various expenses to keep up the Model T.

Mr. Barnes respected the hard work Harold did, as well as the real-life experience he brought. One night an electrician had climbed up a ladder and touched a line, creating a short. Witnessing that the electrician couldn't let go, Harold kicked the ladder out from underneath him. The electrician fell to the floor, jerking him away from the wire and saving his life. Harold learned from Pap and Uncle Pharris this same lesson and told the electrician, "When feeling a wire, use the back of your hand to keep that from happening again." Harold asked for as many hours as possible and sometimes worked sixteen hours a day. What was more, he still had to complete his chores at home. One day he returned home from work to receive a surprise when Edward told him, "I've had to take some of the work off Annie because she is going to have another child." Annie was in her forties, and Harold and Naomi hadn't thought there would be any other children.

Harold looked at Edward and said, "Pap, did you go to sleep with your motor running?"

Edward looked back at Harold while shaking his head and said, "Boy, you ain't got any sense."

Harold walked off chuckling. Annie gave birth months later to a boy they named Roby Joe. Harold helped Annie with the baby when he came home from work so she could rest. He helped give the bottle to Roby Joe and changed and washed the cloth diapers with the washboard.

One evening Annie looked at Harold and startled him with her voice, "Harold, thank you. I hope you know how much I love you. I really appreciate all the help."

Harold responded, "No, Mama, you and Pap have had to work hard to keep us and our farm going. Go rest. Roby Joe will be okay."

In mid-April 1943, Harold's life changed forever. He had received a draft notice to report to the courthouse in Lexington,

North Carolina, on May 3, 1943. Harold drove the Model T and picked up some friends to go to a local dance hall run by Hobert Yarbrough on Highway 29. The crowd walked in, and Harold drank part of a quart of beer. Others bought quarts also and decided to go to Tyro High School to see a play which was debuting. The principal saw the quarts of beer and stopped the group at the door. He yelled at everyone: "Get back in the Model T. Go home and don't wreck!" Taking the principal's advice, Harold got everyone back in the car and delivered them safely home. By this time Harold's beer was too warm to drink. He threw it out.

The next day Harold showed his draft notice to Mr. Barnes. He looked at Harold and said, "I will hold your job until you return from the war." He placed his hand on Harold's shoulder and continued, "Take care of yourself and come back safely."

On the day he reported, Harold and fifty other area men were put on a bus bound for Camp Croft, South Carolina. The men were processed and checked for physical qualities. Harold was just eighteen and felt homesick long before the bus entered South Carolina. One of the fifty riding on that bus was a thirty-year-old fellow draftee who invited Harold to a card game. He asked Harold to pick any card and place it back in the deck. He bet Harold ten dollars that he could find the card. Harold fell for the trick, and, sure enough, the man returned the card Harold had placed and took Harold's ten dollars. This was all the money Harold had. The man looked at Harold and returned the ten dollars with a warning that Harold never forgot,

"Never bet on another man's trick. You're young and haven't been anywhere nor experienced many other people."

"Thank you," said Harold, "and I'll be sure to never forget."

Harold Frank passed the military physical easily and was offered his choice of which branch of service to enter. Harold, standing six feet, two inches tall and weighing 210 pounds, still stark naked from the examination replied, "My dad warned me from the Marines because of bad losses in the Pacific. I can't swim well, so I can't do the Navy. So, I'll go Army."

Harold moved over and stood on the Army footprints, and the Army officer said, "We're proud to have you. Go get dressed."

The fifty men were then returned home via cattle trailer for a two-week furlough. In that time Annie worked to fatten up Harold while he did extra chores to get in better shape. After the two-week furlough, the bus returned to pick up Harold and his friend, Artis Cecil. Artis was from Welcome, North Carolina, which was a small community twelve miles from Harold's home in Tyro. Artis played against Harold in basketball and baseball. The two new recruits were delivered to basic training at Fort Jackson, South Carolina. Their high schools had been rivals, but now Artis and Harold were together for basic—at least for the first day. Their stay at Fort Jackson was brief. The two were called out to join others and told they were soon heading to Camp Shelby, Mississippi.

In May 1943 the two arrived together at Camp Shelby, Mississippi, where they received Army clothing and were placed in barracks with other men. They were told they would be held there temporarily until all new recruits arrived. After that they would be sent to the appropriate regiments. The two were separated into different companies and became part of the reactivated 69th Infantry Division. They were placed in new wooden barracks, each holding one platoon. Harold Frank was in 2nd Platoon, Company L, 271st Infantry under the command of Captain Leonard and Staff Sergeant (SSG) Friday. Both men were seasoned U.S. Army veterans. After the first week of basic, the platoon was called in from training and ordered into formation. Captain Leonard said, "I need volunteers to qualify with a weapon which is the only automatic rifle in an infantry squad." He looked at SSG Friday and continued, "Staff Sergeant, show the men the weapon."

"Yes, sir," SSG Friday replied, "This is the Browning Automatic Rifle. It fires the same .30–06 cartridge you use in the M1 Garand, but from now on you will call it the BAR, as it is a Bad Ass Rifle!" This drew lots of laughter from the men in formation. Friday went on to say, "As an automatic weapon with the ammo magazine fully loaded it weighs twenty pounds, and it can fire several hundred rounds per minute. It is the only automatic in a rifle squad. Who would like to volunteer for a chance to qualify with it?"

Private Frank jumped at the chance. He raised hand and said, "I would, Staff Sergeant."

Friday handed the BAR and manual to PVT (Private) Frank. In a few days PVT Frank became so familiar with the weapon that he could take it apart and put it together in ten minutes while blindfolded. Just as Uncle Pharris taught Harold a few years back, Harold knew every part of the weapon and memorized the essentials in the manual. He was amazed to learn that it fired from a cartridge with fifty-four thousand pounds of pressure per square inch—a lot more than his old 12 gauge. After a few weeks of training with the BAR, PVT Frank excelled with the weapon. He easily passed qualification and was promoted to Private First Class (PFC).

SSG Friday began taking PFC Frank to help train the new recruits on the BAR. On one day of training, PFC Frank gathered up enough ammunition to fill a complete magazine for the BAR. He aimed and fired an entire clip at one time at the distant target held by large sticks. Frank felt a boot on his back as the captain over the range yelled, "You can't hit a target firing a whole mag at a time!"

"Call out to the target score soldiers and see for yourself, sir!" Frank replied.

The officer did. All rounds were in the bull's-eye. "PFC, that was just luck," replied the officer. Another target was put up for PFC Frank, and instead of hitting the silhouette, he shot the stick holding the target in half.

Immediately SSG Friday approached the officer and said "Sir, PFC Frank isn't a regular recruit. He knows what he's doing." The officer nodded and walked away. It turned out that PFC Harold Frank not only qualified with the BAR, but was the top shooter in the 271st Infantry Regiment.

The physical training was easy for PFC Frank, and he was often the pacesetter when the platoon was made to run. Frank was amazed at the recruits from New York and Massachusetts who had never fired a weapon. They struggled to hit any of the targets. Some couldn't hold the weapon correctly and let the M1 beat them to death with kickback. Others returned from the range with black eyes. PFC Frank looked at a new friend, a young private from Tennessee named Dewey Campbell, and asked, "How could any man grow up and never shoot a rifle?"

PVT Campbell looked at Harold and said, "I don't know, but they won't survive long in combat."

Frank looked back at Campbell and replied, "Most of us country boys have been shooting guns since we were six years old. How you gonna train a man to fight, shoot, and care for a M1 firing a .30–06 cartridge that can't figure one end from the other?"

Campbell laughed, hit Frank in his arm, and said, "That's why Sergeant Friday gave you the BAR!"

PFC Frank had become friends with PVT Campbell shortly after arrival at Camp Shelby and soon discovered that Campbell couldn't read or write. Frank began to write letters home for him. Harold wrote that Dewey was a good soldier and an excellent marksman. Campbell approached Frank one evening and said, "Frank, I need your help. I want you to write a letter to my girl back in Tennessee. Now I want you to write everything I say, and I trust you."

"I sure will," Frank replied. "What's her name and what do you want to say?"

The two sat down, and as Harold began to write Dewey said, "Her name is Helen."

"Okay, what do you want me to write?"

"Tell her that I love her and that our training at Camp Shelby is tough, but the Army is making soldiers out of us. I met a good buddy that will be writing for me. His name is Harold, and he is a country boy from North Carolina."

Harold looked up at Dewey, who laughed as Harold wrote, "Southern country boys will always find a way to survive."

PVT Dewey went on to tell Harold to write, "You are the only girl I will ever need, and I miss every kiss. When I see you again I have plenty more to give. I'm saving up some money for us. I'm the best at crap shooting and won money."

Harold looked up and laughed, "You want me to write that?"

"You're damn right. I am. And I'm going to send some of it home," replied Dewey.

The two laughed and Harold continued, "Write me and say anything you want to; it won't matter—I trust Harold. I'm anxious to get home again and hold you in my arms. I love you."

PFC Frank wrote and signed the letter for PVT Dewey Campbell. A week later she wrote him back. Campbell received the letter at mail call and later had Harold read it back.

She said: "Dewey darling, I love you too and miss you every day. When you come home we will make love again. I miss you so much, but I'm glad you have made such a good friend. Do you have any idea when you will get some leave to come home? Most of the other boys around here are gone now fighting. You have always been the only one for me and I miss you dearly. I'm waiting for your return. I love you."

Dewey just sat there motionless for a minute and said, "I miss her more than anything. Thanks, Frank. Let's go to the PX and get a beer. I'll pay for it." The letters continued back and forth throughout basic.

PVT Campbell could shoot craps and win most of the time. He would hold dice in the palm of his hand, roll the dice, and throw them when his hands came up near his mouth. He spent some of the money on beer, more on peanuts at the Army PX. He only shared his table with PFC Frank and a few other Southern "country" boys at the Army PX. Harold noticed he could fight like the devil with a knife, bayonet, or gun, but would pass out at the sight of a needle. When the boys lined up to receive shots, Dewey looked at Harold and said, "Get ready to catch me."

Harold replied, "You ain't going to run, are you?"

"No, just pass out," he replied.

Sure enough, as soon as the medic stuck him with a needle, PVT Dewey fell to the floor.

The group of rebel boys became close. On several occasions the Northern boys tried to join their ranks but were refused—except on one occasion when all the 271st men in the PX were called to fight.

A soldier from the 442nd Regimental Combat Team, which was made up entirely of Japanese Americans, stated to the men of the 271st that "This PX was ours" and to "stay away from now on." A fight instantly ensued, and PFC Frank, PVT Dewey, and the boys of the 271st, both Yankees and Rebels, fought the

442nd Regiment. The 271st outnumbered them two-to-one, but the struggle lasted for some time and finally, through fistfights and wrestling, the 271st muscled the boys of the 442nd out the doors and windows. Amazingly, no military police had arrived. Harold yelled through the window while catching his breath and looking at PVT Campbell, "Y'all can fight good, but go hunt another PX." They never bothered the 271st again. Sadly for Campbell and Frank, after basic they would never see each other again. PFC Frank would be transferred along with other BAR men in preparation for D-Day.

PFC Frank's only major obstacle while in basic and advanced training was the battle with the "leaves of three" otherwise known as poison oak. The first encounter happened during an overnight bivouac where he came into contact with the plant. It was dark and raining when the men were ordered to rest for the night. The next morning Frank had broken out in copious sores and blisters. He went to the infirmary to get care from the unit medics. Treatment included being covered with calamine lotion and having thin bandages wrapped around areas of puss and blisters. Several days of discomfort followed along with the temptation to scratch for relief—while fearing that doing so would cause the further spread of rashes. Harold recovered and was promptly placed back in his platoon where he remained free of the leaves of three for the duration of basic training.

The second obstacle occurred during advanced infantry training. During night maneuvers, PFC Frank was ordered to dig a firing position in a large area of poison oak. He looked at the sergeant and down at rich, healthy growths of the leaves of three. Harold said, "Sergeant, I'm badly affected by poison oak."

"Doesn't matter, Private. You dig here not because of poison oak but to be in the right position to support the platoon in case of attack," the sergeant replied.

In the morning PFC Frank had broken out so badly he was immediately taken to the Camp Shelby Field Hospital where he received immediate attention. He was covered in calamine lotion and bandages and had to be washed daily by the Army nurses. For two days the rashes and swelling caused his eyes to remain shut. The next day the swelling in Harold's face subsided and his sight was restored. One of the nurses was especially attractive and attempted to change the bandages and apply lotion along his waist and between his legs. This resulted in an embarrassing arousal. The nurse stopped, looked at PFC Frank, and said, "Private, after this time you will need to clean yourself."

PFC Frank replied, "Yes ma'am, sorry."

"There's nothing to be sorry about," she responded while applying more calamine to the sores on his side before walking away.

After she left the room, several other soldiers laughed. Frank raised his calamine covered arms and said, "What? I couldn't help it." Everyone laughed again, including Frank.

After returning to his unit, it became apparent that October was the month for intense combat training. Bivouacking at this point consisted of digging and sleeping in foxholes. Simulated combat dominated the training. It included digging holes in the morning before moving out during live-fire training, and at night falling back and finding the same foxhole from the previous day. The rigorous training lasted for several weeks, and the food was at best only C-rations. After three weeks the men of L Company were ordered back to camp to rest and get a shower. PFC Frank was walking back from the latrine and noticed a wild hog trapped in a garbage pit. The cook's tent was nearby. The mess sergeant looked at PFC Frank and said, "If you kill it and gut it, I'll fix it just for the soldiers in L Company, 271st Infantry. No officers will know because they wouldn't approve."

"You give me an axe and a butcher knife, and I'll do it," Frank replied.

The mess sergeant disappeared into the tent and came back in a minute with a sharpened axe and knife. Frank jumped into the eight-by-eight pit with the axe, and the hog moved toward him. With just one swing he hit the beast above his eyes. The hog rolled over, and, just as in hog killing back home, PFC Frank quickly stuck the hog through the neck to heart and let the animal bleed out. Other men from L Company saw what was happening and began cheering and laughing. PVT Dewey Campbell and PFC Leon White yelled, "Good job, Frank! We'll help you get him out." Other men climbed down and gave Frank a rope to tie around the hog so that the men could hoist the hog out. The Southern boys quickly helped Harold skin the hog. There was no time for scalding since everyone was hungry. The mess sergeant came up with pots and said, "Glad to see a few country boys. We'll have a feast tonight. Just wait till you hear me blow a whistle, then bring the company into the mess tent."

Frank left the mess tent and told the company to put in a contribution to buy beer at the PX. The money flowed in, and that night when the mess sergeant blew a whistle, L Company piled into the mess tent to chow down on whole-hog chopped barbecue accompanied by ice-cold beer. Everyone celebrated and came over to the table where PVT Campbell, PFC White, and PFC Frank sat, patting them on the shoulder.

Other country boys said, "Next time y'all kill a hog, let us know and we'll help."

After supper the mess sergeant walked up to PFC Frank and said, "You did a good job killing that hog. Where did you learn to do that?"

"Back home we had to kill lots of hogs. If not, my family would've gone hungry," Frank replied.

After completing their combat training one day, L Company was returning to the main camp when a jeep drove by. SSG Friday stopped and yelled, "PFC Frank, need to see you."

PFC Frank walked over to the jeep, and SSG Friday said, "Hop in." He looked at Frank and said, "Don't tell anyone, but let's go to town. You got some money?"

Frank said, "Sure do, let's go."

The two drove off into the night using only blackout lights and disappeared into the Mississippi woods at top speed. The jeep came into a small town just before stores closed. Friday and Frank went into a store and bought some real candy bars: Baby

Ruth, Butterfingers, and Mounds—plus a few bottles of coke. The men chowed down on the contraband before heading back to camp. No one knew the men had been gone.

In December of 1943, PFC Frank and the men of his platoon graduated from Infantry Training. SSG Friday sent for PFC Frank to enter the company orderly room. When Frank arrived, Sergeant Friday, Lieutenant Statler, and Captain Leonard were standing around the Captain's desk.

Captain Leonard looked at Frank standing at attention and said, "At ease PFC, Sergeant Friday has something to ask you."

Friday looked at Frank and said, "Congratulations with basic. You are an expert with the BAR, the best in the 271st. We would like for you to remain here at Camp Shelby and help us train new recruits on the weapon. If you choose to do so the captain is working on getting you promoted to corporal. You will have to go through one more school however, called ASTP [Advanced Specialized Training Program]. Do you want the position?"

Frank looked from Friday to Captain Leonard and stated, "I didn't join the Army to go to school. I came here to kill Germans and Japs."

The captain looked at Friday, then at Frank and said, "Thank you, PFC. You are a good soldier and a hell of a BAR rifleman. You're dismissed."

PFC Frank returned to his platoon, and the following day the 271st began a ninety-five-mile road march to Gulfport, Mississippi, to complete amphibious training. It was a long training exercise taking several days. The 271st had just completed the march and was taking a break when an officer arrived by jeep. He stood up and the order was given to fall in. When the men formed up, the officer yelled, "If your name is called, fall out and report to me." PFC Frank was one of the names he called, and as Harold started towards the officer, he noticed all the men were BAR qualifiers. An Army truck pulled up and the men were put in trucks and driven back to Camp Shelby.

After they had unloaded from the truck, an officer approached the men and said, "Tomorrow is Friday. You all have been given a three-day pass. Make sure you are here Monday morning at 0600. If you're late, you will be considered AWOL. Have a good weekend." The men were then dismissed.

A fellow BAR soldier and friend, PFC Leon White, came up to PFC Frank and said, "Never saw that officer before."

"Me neither," Frank replied while scratching his chin.

Leon looked at Harold and said, "How would you like to come to my farm in Temple, Georgia? It's not far."

"I'll go," Harold replied.

Both left that Friday by train to enjoy the rare pass, but clueless as to why they'd received it.

White's farm was not on a regular stop for the Southern Railroad, so as the two boarded the train PFC White asked the conductor, "Can you stop near Temple, Georgia? We've got a three-day pass, and I'd like to see home one last time."

The conductor replied, "I'll stop when the emergency brake is pulled and let you two off."

"Will you stop at the same place Sunday?" White asked.

"I'll be coming through Sunday at the same time," the conductor said.

"Stop and pick us up at the same time," said White, "or we will be considered AWOL."

"I'll be here, and you boys be careful."

As the train neared Temple, White pulled the emergency brake. The train slowed to a stop, and the two soldiers left the train track and walked the half mile or so to the farm. Harold enjoyed meeting Leon's family. The following morning the two had a real country breakfast and Leon said to Harold, "Let's go to a movie and a late dinner." The only town with a theater close by was Valdosta, Georgia. White called his girlfriend and asked if she could go, and he suggested she bring Virginia Dobbs, his cousin.

The two girls arrived, and Virginia ran up to meet PFC Frank. Harold noticed that she was attractive, even though she was a brunette (Harold had a particular fondness for red hair). "I like you, Virginia," Harold said. "Would you go with us to the movies?"

"I sure would," she said.

Leon borrowed his brother's car, and they left for town.

They arrived at the theatre and bought some drinks and popcorn before entering the theatre. They found some seats towards the back. As the movie began Virginia whispered to Harold, "So do you have a girlfriend in North Carolina?"

Harold, sounding a little nervous, tried to whisper his answer, but his voice had trouble, "No, there was never time. All I knew was work and survival."

Virginia held his hand and felt the calluses of a country boy. She said, "Guess the Depression was hard on us all. Hopefully it is over." They looked into each other's eyes and kissed. At first it was a little awkward, but Frank placed his hand around Virginia's waist, and she allowed him to draw her close. No one afterwards could recall the name of the movie, but Harold and Virginia enjoyed getting to know one another.

After the movie they ate dinner at a local store in Valdosta that served barbecue. They all returned home after dark. Leon's first stop was Virginia's house. Harold walked her to the doorway and kissed her goodnight.

"I like you," Virginia said. She then paused and looked into Harold's eyes. "Harold, many boys have gone and will never come home. You can see it in the windows of families that I know and that scares me." Hitting Harold on the chest, she continued, "I'm not going to cry, but you be careful and come back when the war is over." Looking at Leon who was still waiting in the car, Virginia sighed and said, "I hope all you boys win this war and come home. Take care of yourself, you hear?"

Harold nodded and said, "Honey, thank you, and some day when this war is over, I'd like to see you again."

The couple kissed one last time and Harold returned to the car. With both girls dropped off at their homes, Harold got in the passenger seat and hit Leon on the arm, laughed, and said, "Thank you. Your cousin is something special."

The two rested that night. On Sunday morning they headed back to the railroad track. Sure enough, the conductor was right on time.

"Did you boys have a good weekend?" the conductor asked.

"Yes, sir, and thank you," Harold replied.

After reporting back to Camp Shelby, they were told they were heading overseas but were first going by troop train to Fort Meade, Maryland. In Fort Meade, PFC Frank used a phone for the first time to call his sister Naomi, who had moved to Lexington. She shared an apartment with another friend while working to make military equipment. In a letter to Harold, she had mentioned that she had a phone. Frank entered the Fort Meade PX and asked how to use a pay phone.

A soldier said, "Go get some quarters, nickels, and dimes. Then at the pay phone dial the O and wait on the operator."

Harold walked up to a pay telephone, dialed the operator, and said, "I'm a dumbass and don't know how to use a phone, but I'm trying to call home."

The operator laughed and said, "I'll help you through this." She dialed his sister in Lexington, North Carolina.

Naomi answered and PFC Frank said, "This is your brother Harold. I'm in Fort Meade, Maryland, and preparing to head overseas and getting our shots. Get ahold of Momma and Daddy and tell them."

She replied, "I hope you don't go overseas, and what do you mean by shots?"

"To keep us from disease or getting sick," Harold said.

"I'll tell them."

"I love you and I'll see you when I come back home. Bye."

The operator told Harold how much to put in the coin slot on the pay phone. Harold said to the operator, "Thank you for helping me."

"Thank you. It's my job," the operator said.

CHAPTER 8

One Last Visit and Staff Sergeant Frisco

O n a Saturday at 0530, PFC Frank was awakened and told to go to the orderly room. Startled and concerned, he ran out across the grass where soldiers were not allowed to run and was caught by the commanding officer who shouted, "You'll be on KP till you leave here, but your parents are waiting on you in the day room."

As soon as he walked in, his parents caught him up in a hug before asking, "Can you leave the base?"

"I don't know. I'll have to ask the CO," replied Harold.

Harold walked to the commanding officer's office to talk to the soldier on duty. "Sergeant, I'm PFC Frank and request to talk with the CO. My folks arrived and ask if I can leave the post."

The sergeant replied, "Stay here," and knocked on the CO's door. Upon receiving the order to enter, the sergeant relayed Frank's request.

The CO walked out and said, "PFC Frank, yes you can leave the base, but be back before reveille."

"Can I be kept off KP until after my parents go home?" Frank asked.

"Okay, PFC, but be back before reveille Monday morning."

"Yes, sir, I'm not a deserter," Frank replied.

On Saturday, the Frank family visited the National Mall and the Tomb of the Unknown Soldier in Washington, D.C.

Edward told Harold they had been able to travel to Fort Meade by train since their cousin Mr. Young worked for the railroad as a conductor and lived nearby in Spencer, North Carolina. They'd caught the train in Lexington and traveled all the way to Fort Meade on it. On Sunday before daylight, the Franks continued the tour at Union Station and ran into Alan Swicegood. They knew Swicegood from Tyro. He walked up and asked, "Why are y'all here?" PFC Frank told Alan about preparing to go overseas and the sudden arrival of his parents.

Alan replied, "I'll take the day off and show you all around."

Alan took them back to the Washington Monument, Harold's favorite, then to the Tomb of the Unknown Soldier. Along the way they ate lunch. PFC Frank took in the sights and listened to Alan as he pointed out each of the national shrines.

Harold looked at everyone and said, "Washington is a very clean city and as safe as being on the farm. Hope it stays that way. Thanks for coming and showing me around."

"It's my pleasure," Swicegood replied. Then he shook Harold's hand and looked at his parents and said, "Your boy is something special, and, with prayer, I feel he will come back safe."

That evening Edward and Annie rode the train back to Lexington, and PFC Frank went by Metro to Fort Meade. Before final goodbyes, Edward looked at Harold and said, "Son, you don't know what you're heading in for. I've taught you everything I know."

"Yes, sir," replied Harold.

Edward put his hand on Harold's shoulder, looked into Harold's eyes and said, "You can drive anything, fix anything, and out work anyone. Your Uncle Pharris and I taught you to shoot, hunt, and survive on very little. No matter the danger, remember to keep the faith. If you take care of the equipment, it will take care of you. Take care of yourself and come back safe." Edward hugged his son.

Harold turned to his mother, and Annie said, "I love you, Harold. Never forget this." She paused, holding back tears, then said, "I will never stop praying for you. Night or day, I'll be in prayer, and every time I hear news from the war, I'll say another prayer. You come back to me. You hear me?"

Harold nodded and said, "I know you'll be praying, and I love you too."

Edward and Annie watched through tears as their son walked away. Then his parents walked to the train and headed back to Lexington.

The next morning PFC Frank was on KP but only for the day. Frank made a new acquaintance in Frisco, a Regular Army sergeant who was shorter than Harold and stood about five feet, ten inches tall. The two became friends and for the next two weeks went through training with the gas mask and M1 Garand. Frank and Frisco were in different platoons. Frisco introduced himself as being from "San Fran California Frisco," thus earning the nickname "Frisco." One night Frisco came into the barracks at midnight. He was drunk and he quickly grabbed a fire extinguisher. He then proceeded to spray everybody in the barracks as they awakened. It took PFC Frank and three others to subdue him. They all laughed with a few cussing about being awakened at 0100. Later that morning Frisco approached Harold with a dilemma. Frisco's aunt had wired him two hundred dollars, but his unit was suddenly placed on alert, so he couldn't cash it. He gave Harold the wire, his dog tags, and his GI driver's license. Frank's unit was not yet on alert, so Frisco asked Harold to run to the Western Union *seventeen blocks* away and get the money.

Frank ran the distance and walked in, giving the clerk Frisco's information. He was impersonating Frisco. The clerk gave Frank the money, and he ran the seventeen blocks back in less than two hours; but by the time he arrived, Frisco's unit was gone. Frank took everything to the first sergeant who sent him to the CO's office. He saluted the CO before explaining the situation. PFC Frank looked at the captain, "What can I do? I don't want to keep his money."

"Put everything in an envelope," the captain said, "and I'll find out where the unit went and send the envelope."

"You be sure to send it to him because he trusted me to do this," Frank insisted.

"I will find out and get it to him," the captain said.

The next morning PFC Frank's group went on alert before embarking on the on-troop train to Camp Shanks, New York. At Camp Shanks, Frank checked into his new barracks. Then he went alone to the PX and bought a beer. As Frank sat down, he heard his name called out and turned to see Sergeant Frisco rushing over and exclaiming, "Where is my money? I'm broke." Frank bought Frisco a beer and told him the story, including the captain's statement.

Frisco paused and said, "Don't worry about it. I trust you and don't worry about it anymore."

The two drank their beer before Sergeant Frisco departed. As he was leaving, he said "It'll show up."

After a brief training session, they boarded troop ships bound for Scotland. As with so many other soldiers he met, Frank never saw Frisco again.

CHAPTER 9

PFC Esworthy and Joe Lewis: Harold Becomes a Cook!

Once on board the ship to Scotland, PFC Frank and the company of soldiers with him were guided to their bunks. Harold felt uneasy about combat preparations. As a BAR rifleman, he couldn't fix a bayonet on the end of the rifle. He asked a couple of soldiers around him what they were carrying.

A corporal chimed in, "They have Case double-bladed hunting knives in the ship store."

Harold hollered, "Thanks, that what I need."

Harold and several other men went to the ship store and returned with a Case six-inch, double-bladed hunting knife. Harold returned to his bunk feeling relieved and noticed that others preparing for combat had similar backup weapons. While the soldiers were unpacking gear and resting in their bunks, a sergeant holding a clipboard appeared.

"Listen up, cooks!" he shouted. Harold could barely hear him and was hurrying to put away his new weapon. The sergeant held up a clipboard and said, "Answer out if you hear your name." Harold moved close as names were uttered. He heard the sergeant say, "Frank."

Immediately, Harold yelled back, "Here, Sergeant."

Once the roll of names was completed the sergeant said, "You all are the cooks." Harold looked around confused but quiet. Then the sergeant called out a second list and yelled out "Frank" once again.

Harold turned as another soldier replied, "Here, Sergeant."

Afterwards the sergeant said, "You all are the KP."

Harold smiled and thought, "Since I'm a cook, I can tell the KP what to do. However, what in the world can I cook?"

The sergeant ordered the cooks to follow him. They walked out into an open area, and the sergeant asked, "Which meal do you all prefer to fix?"

Harold quickly yelled, "Breakfast!" because it was the one regular meal that PFC Frank felt he could cook.

The sergeant looked and said, "Frank, right?"

"Yes, Sergeant," Harold replied.

The sergeant continued, "Okay, report to the kitchen at 0500. You can return below deck."

Harold left happy but concerned. The next morning as the cooks and KP arrived for duty, a soldier who also had the last name Frank came up and asked, "Are you a cook?"

"Yes, that's why they called me," Harold replied.

The other Frank retorted, "Well, I'm a cook also and shouldn't be on KP."

At 0500 PFC Frank reported to the kitchen to begin breakfast. The mess sergeant looked at the cooks and said, "We will fix six hundred dozen eggs.

"That's a hell of a lot of eggs!" Frank exclaimed, and several of the men chuckled in agreement.

"Don't matter," said the mess sergeant, "that's how many it takes."

He showed Frank the equipment, each of the containers, and the steam cooker to be used for the eggs. The steam cooker had an on-and-off switch that heated up the pot, and an automatic stirrer scrambled the eggs. The mess sergeant looked at Frank and asked, "PFC, do you think you can handle this?"

"Yes, Sergeant. It's no problem. I've fixed many a breakfast," replied Frank.

He thought, "This isn't too bad. I can do it regardless of not being a cook." He smiled at the KP and began his impression of being a cook.

Frank looked at the KPs and ordered, "Privates, get the eggs and bring them to the kitchen." After a few minutes, six KPs returned, and Frank ordered, "Break the eggs carefully and don't let the shells get into the container." None of the KPs suspected that he wasn't a cook, so they did just as he ordered. Frank had a good laugh before he said, "Good job, Privates. I don't see any eggshells. Go ahead and dump them into the cooker." Frank knew that he liked scrambled eggs soft, not overcooked, so he watched the cooker stir until the eggs looked just right. Then Frank ordered one of the KPs to dish out some of the scrambled eggs so that he could sample them. "They're perfect," Frank declared. He told the KPs, "Turn off the cooker and pour the scrambled eggs into the stainless-steel pans." Quickly the KPs poured the eggs into pans. Each pan would serve fifty men. At the same time, Frank ordered another KP to bring up the link sausage that the KP had set out to thaw. PFC Frank ordered the KPs to dump the links into the next cooker. He watched to make sure the sausages were thoroughly cooked, then said, "Step back!" He picked out three sausage links and ate them. "Very good," he proclaimed. "Go ahead and dip the links out. Put them into the pans and bring them out to the serving line with the eggs."

The mess sergeant came by and said, "PFC, you're doing good. You've done this a lot."

Frank laughed and said, "Thank you, Sergeant. I'm trying to do the best I can."

The sergeant walked over to the ovens warming the breakfast rolls and said, "PFC, send over a KP and I'll get the rolls."

"Yes, Sergeant!" Frank replied.

He eyed one of the privates and said, "You heard the sergeant, give 'em some help." Soon the KPs brought each pan to the serving line. The soldiers were already lined up at 0630, hungry for breakfast.

The KPs were stationed at the chow line to dish out the morning meal. Each soldier picked up a tray, which had four slots for food. One KP would dish out the eggs and another the sausage, while the third placed a roll on each tray as the soldiers passed, all under Frank's supervision. Frank's bunkmate PFC Paul Esworthy from Frederick, Maryland, was near the front of the line and saw Frank supervising the KP but didn't say anything. Later that morning when Frank made it back and crawled into his bunk, Esworthy, who was on the upper bunk got up and said, "I didn't know you were a cook."

Frank looked around and said, "Shhhh...I'm not. I'm a BAR rifleman in the infantry, but I don't want to be on KP. Somehow, they had a mix up and placed me as the cook. Another guy by the name of Frank said he was the cook, but they put him on KP."

Esworthy laughed and said, "I'll keep it a secret, but when I get called for KP, I just want to be on the serving line."

"All right," Harold said, and laid back on the bed with a smile. Thankfully, nothing else was ever said. Amazingly, after the second day, Frank thought, "No one complained of my cooking." Perhaps that was partly due to being on a Liberty Ship with no regular cooks.

The ship was a rough ride causing many to get sick, including Frank. He became sick the first day before leaving sight of New York. The lower decks were tightly compacted with bunks four high and down the sides and then through the middle of the ship. A small aisle separated the bunks, with Frank's being the third one up. Each morning after a 10:00 breakfast, Frank's ship section was ordered onto the top deck. A group of staff sergeants ordered the men, "Strip off to your skivvies. It's time for exercise." "Side, straddle, hop" (or "jumping jacks" in the civilian world) combined with arm twists followed by lots of push-ups. The exercises were intense for thirty minutes. Then the men were ordered to attention and sent back below deck as other sections reported up for exercise. Each day the men had classes on Allied and Nazi weapons including tanks, artillery, and airplanes. No one impressed upon them that they were preparing for D-Day, but Frank felt something was special about the men on this ship. After each class, the men were constantly inspected, and boots had to be shined. Their remaining time was spent playing cards, especially poker or "five-card stud." Frank and Esworthy were talked into playing with two soldiers, one from Missouri and the other from Pennsylvania, who both said to them, "Look, we all know we're going to lead the invasion of France and most likely we'll get killed. We may never see money or home again, so let's play poker."

"I'm game," Frank replied.

PFC Esworthy jumped off the bunk and said, "Deal me in."

"All right, gentlemen," replied the Pennsylvanian, "five-card stud, joker's wild, and a dollar bet on opening pair. You can raise a dollar."

PFC Frank enjoyed the card playing, especially after returning from "cooking." Frank struggled with the game at first, but perhaps since becoming a "cook" instead of KP, Frank felt he had discovered a new talent: he excelled in bluffing. Many soldiers came over to watch Frank play, and by the time the ship had arrived in England, Frank had made fifty dollars—a huge sum for a PFC.

On March 23, 1944, fourteen days after departure, the ships docked in Glasgow, Scotland. They waited there until troop trains arrived to take them to the tent cities. The tent cities were set up to prepare and train the troops for the D-Day invasion. At the time Frank and the others didn't know there was going to be a D-Day invasion, of course. Frank and several other BAR soldiers were pulled from the group and transferred to a training area with the 90th Division, known as the "Tough Hombres." They would be the replacements following the initial waves of soldiers preparing for the invasion of France. Each day the soldiers completed forced marches while carrying heavy loads along with their weapons and ammo. The goal was for the soldiers to complete a forced march of five miles in less than an hour. In their spare time they did calisthenics, took classes, and went to the range.

On April 1, 1944, a staff sergeant came into the tent where Frank, Esworthy, and six other soldiers were bunked. The staff sergeant held a clipboard and yelled, "PFC Frank."

Frank looked up and said, "Yes, Staff Sergeant."

The staff sergeant put the clipboard down and said, "I understand you are a 746 [BAR riflemen] and that you were with the 271st Infantry in the 69th Division at Camp Shelby and that you're a Tar Heel. You rebels make good riflemen." With a grin he hesitated but then looked at Frank and added, "Do you remember a Sergeant Friday?"

"Yes," Frank replied. "He trained me with the BAR and later had me help train other new recruits."

The staff sergeant laughed and said, "I know him. A good man but scared shitless of snakes!"

Frank laughed and said, "Oh, Lordy, on one of our maneuvers we were bivouacked in the same shelter half tent and a middle-sized black snake slivered over his boots. He raised up, yelled, and took off carrying the tent, pegs and all. I woke up looking at the stars and turned to see him collide into a live oak." All eight soldiers in the tent erupted in laughter. Frank looked at everyone and said, "I just looked up at the stars and said, 'Oh, Lordy, Lordy!'"

After a few minutes, the staff sergeant said, "Frank, I'm here to get you and take you to the range to help train others with the BAR. Who is your assistant gunner, or do I need to find someone?"

Esworthy raised his hand and said, "I'll volunteer."

"It's done then. You two be ready at 0600," said the staff sergeant.

Then before leaving the tent, he looked at Frank and stated, "PFC, we need as many experienced BAR men as possible to help train these replacements."

"If anyone can do it, I know I can," Frank replied.

The men all looked at each other as the staff sergeant left the tent.

As Frank trained with his new assistant gunner, PFC Paul Esworthy, they became close friends. During this time the reality of war became more apparent, so Frank and Esworthy watched, learned, trained, and slept preparing for the coming invasion.

Frank and Esworthy were informed they would be replacements brought in following the first waves of attack. They still did not know what beach they would be sent to. In the meantime, they completed training near Newport, Wales, for the D-Day invasion. They attended classes where they discussed how they would land but not the exact beaches. During the afternoon they practiced shooting. Frank brought out his BAR, and as soon as he shot, he caught the attention of the soldiers training to be replacements. All lacked the marksmanship ability that Harold Frank displayed.

In early May, the training slacked off enough for Frank to get several days of rest. He borrowed a bicycle and rode into a nearby English village, where he noticed the beautiful countryside covered in bright green pastures. The sight of the livestock and farm smells assuaged some of Frank's home sickness. He walked into a small pub and ordered some fish and chips with a mug a beer. A young woman walked over and asked, "Can I sit with you for a minute?"

"Yes, you can," Frank replied. "Sit here beside me." The woman was about five feet, five inches with sandy blonde hair and a good figure.

Harold said, "Let me buy you some fish and chips and a beer."

"Okay," she said, and Harold ordered. "Tell me where you are from and what you did back home," the young lady said to Harold.

"I'm from Tyro, North Carolina. Grew up dirt poor in a

Lutheran family and farmed for a living. We grew cotton, sweet potatoes, and various grains."

She asked, "I bet you miss being home? Do you have brothers and sisters?"

"Yes, two brothers and two sisters." He laughed and added, "My sister Naomi is two years older than me and could also always out-pick me in the cotton field."

The English woman smiled and said, "My family raise sheep. You should have noticed that as you came into this village from the tent city where you Yanks are training."

Frank laughed and said, "I'm not a Yank. I'm from North Carolina."

She looked at Harold, confused, and with a grin he said, "You wouldn't understand, but my family were Rebels during the War between the States."

She sat back with a serious look and said, "I've heard about that. You boys lost?"

"Well, we don't like to talk about it anymore. The Great Depression took care of that," he replied. With a long pause Frank looked at the young lady and said, "Just surviving as a country boy."

She responded, "We survived the Depression but had it really hard in 1940. The Blitz killed some of my family, and several others are getting ready for the big invasion like you."

After they had eaten Harold asked, "Can we see the farm?"

The two walked out of the pub to her farm on a picturesque green hillside. Off in the distance she pointed out the sheep grazing. She had a blanket and the two sat down. After a few minutes she moved closer to Harold and the two kissed, hugged, and began removing clothes. They had just about figured each other out when another soldier from Frank's camp went by on his bike whistling and laughing while waving at the girl. The mood changed and Frank said, "I've got to get back."

"You come back," she said.

After a parting kiss, Frank looked around and located the bike and whistling soldier as he thought to himself, "I think she has seen a few others from camp." He left and headed on back to tent city.

Frank began helping train other soldiers, a fact that created jealousy in another staff sergeant. After a few days, some of the men began listening to Frank. One evening the staff sergeant said to Frank, "Let's box tomorrow evening."

Frank replied, "No."

Each day the staff sergeant persisted until Frank said, "Okay. Let's box."

The two put on boxing gloves, and after the sergeant hit Frank with several jabs, Frank lowered his glove. When the staff sergeant swung again, Frank hit back hard, connecting with the center of his head and knocking the staff sergeant down. As he came around for another blow, the staff sergeant said, "No more."

In May 1944 the boxer Joe Lewis came in a driving rainstorm to speak to the men as part of the United Service Organizations (USO). Many waited in the tent city with excitement to see the boxer, but after an hour the clouds overhead became a driving rainstorm. Lewis finally emerged from an Army-green four-door car. He walked up to the stage and said, "How you soldiers doing in this rain?" Frank and Esworthy were upset at having to stand out in the rain for so long.

Frank looked at Esworthy and asked, "We stood out here in the rain for a five-minute speech?"

Esworthy shook his head and said, "I agree. Let's go back to the tent and get some dry clothes."

CHAPTER 10

D-Day to Gourbesville:
Rendezvous with the 357th Infantry

O n June 1, 1944, main elements began loading on nine transport ships at Newport to sail to Dartmouth, England. Group A remained in Dartmouth while other advanced elements sailed on the USS *Susan B. Anthony*. Frank remembered all the training, and as the men loaded on the troop ships, they thought that all were ready to fight and end this war and get home.

On June 4 much of the 357th, 358th, and 359th Infantry Regiments loaded on three LSTs [Landing Ship, Tank]—*Excelsior* at Newport, *Explorer* at Cardiff, and *Bienville* at Cardiff)—in Southampton. On June 6, well before dawn, word arrived that the invasion was on. A first sergeant passed the word that the ships were finally departing for France. The Normandy invasions would be continuous. To avoid the disaster that happened during the Raid on Dieppe, France, two years earlier, new strategies had

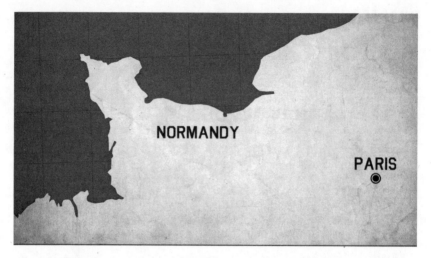

Normandy—Paris. *Courtesy of Brannon Judd and Pritchett Cotten*

been devised. Back then, over four thousand Canadian soldiers had been either killed or captured trying to take the coastal town of Dieppe. Bad intelligence placed the invasion on beaches that couldn't support tanks or trucks. Furthermore, there was a lack of adequate air support and no plan for disrupting German reinforcements from reinforcing the shore defenses. Dieppe was a disaster. Normandy would be a different matter. Hopefully.

Allied airborne units would jump during the night to secure key crossroads, bridges, and high ground. The goal was to secure and hold their assigned positions till the seaborne infantry landed, secured the causeways, and made contact with the airborne invasion force. The main Normandy seaport of Cherbourg would be sidestepped and then cut off. It would be taken by attacking across

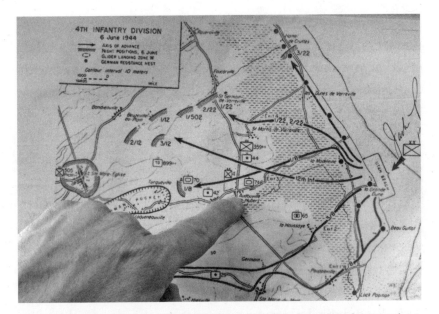

Sylvain Kast points to the rendezvous point of the 357th Infantry where
Harold joined

the Cotentin Peninsula instead of from the water. Key cities in
Normandy had to be taken to allow for the invasion to move deep
into Europe. The cities of Caen, Carentan, Sainte Mère Église, and
especially Saint-Lô had to be secured to capture Normandy.
Saint-Lô was the main goal. Division after division would hit five
different beaches on consecutive days and weeks. Each reinforcing
group was to pass through the peninsula, relieving battle-worn
units and pressing the attack until all of Normandy was secure.
During each wave, replacements landed to be quickly transferred
into combat based on specific skill sets. PFC Frank, being a BAR
rifleman, could expect immediate action.

The men marched in columns of four to board the transports. On the way, Frank noticed that the Red Cross sold a coffee and doughnut for ten cents. Frank looked at Esworthy in disgust and said, "We're on our way to fight and die and they want us to *buy* that! If I survive, I'll never forgot this."

Most of the replacements stared in disbelief as they passed by the Red Cross. After a halt, the soldiers began loading onto the LST.

Esworthy nodded to Frank and said, "Well, looks like there was no takers for the cup of joe."

Frank glanced back and, while adjusting his web gear and BAR, replied, "Oh, Lordy, it ain't right."

PFC Frank and PFC Esworthy boarded the LST. Their transport vessel carried six tanks with infantry squads on either side. The sailing route would be from Bristol Channel to France. It had been several days since the initial landing, but the relentless roar of aircraft headed across the Channel filled the sky. Frank and Esworthy looked up into the darkness as huge numbers of Allied planes screamed by overhead. The sound was deafening. Frank grabbed Esworthy's shoulder and shouted, "Give 'em hell, boys!" Esworthy let out a rebel yell, and the two were joined by others in the company as they watched and listened. The overhead flights did not diminish; the sky remained filled with Allied planes of all types. Frank looked at Esworthy and yelled loudly enough to be heard over the roar of planes. Finally, there was enough silence to hear someone else speak. A first sergeant held up a piece of paper and said, "Gather around and take a knee.

This was handed to me to read. Listen up! This was read to the men who we all saw go before us. Now it's our turn."

SUPREME HEADQUARTERS
ALLIED EXPEDITIONARY FORCE

Soldiers, Sailors and Airmen of the Allied Expeditionary Force!

You are about to embark upon the Great Crusade, toward which we have striven these many months. The eyes of the world are upon you. The hopes and prayers of liberty-loving people everywhere march with you. In company with our brave Allies and brothers-in-arms on other Fronts, you will bring about the destruction of the German war machine, the elimination of Nazi tyranny over the oppressed peoples of Europe, and security for ourselves in a free world.

Your task will not be an easy one. Your enemy is well trained, well equipped and battle hardened. He will fight savagely.

But this is the year 1944! Much has happened since the Nazi triumphs of 1940-41. The United Nations have inflicted upon the Germans great defeats, in open battle, man-to-man. Our air offensive has seriously reduced their strength in the air and their capacity to wage war on the ground. Our Home Fronts have given us an overwhelming superiority in weapons and munitions of war, and placed at our disposal great reserves of trained fighting men. The tide has turned! The free men of the world are marching together to Victory!

I have full confidence in your courage, and devotion to duty and skill in battle. We will accept nothing less than full Victory!

Good luck! And let us beseech the blessing of Almighty God upon this great and noble undertaking.

SIGNED: Dwight D. Eisenhower[1]

In the United States, the Franks turned on the radio to hear the President's call for prayer. D-Day was commencing. Edward, Annie, Naomi, and untold others prayed as they listened to FDR's words.

My fellow Americans: Last night, when I spoke with you about the fall of Rome, I knew at that moment that troops of the United States and our allies were crossing the Channel in another and greater operation. It has come to pass with success thus far.

And so, in this poignant hour, I ask you to join with me in prayer:

Almighty God: Our sons, pride of our Nation, this day have set upon a mighty endeavor, a struggle to preserve our Republic, our religion, and our civilization, and to set free a suffering humanity.

Lead them straight and true; give strength to their arms, stoutness to their hearts, steadfastness in their faith.

They will need Thy blessings. Their road will be long and hard. For the enemy is strong. He may hurl back our forces. Success may not come with rushing speed, but we shall return again and again; and we know that by Thy grace, and by the righteousness of our cause, our sons will triumph.

They will be sore tried, by night and by day, without rest—until the victory is won. The darkness will be rent by noise and flame. Men's souls will be shaken with the violences of war.

For these men are lately drawn from the ways of peace. They fight not for the lust of conquest. They fight to end conquest. They fight to liberate. They fight to let justice arise, and tolerance and good will among all Thy people. They yearn but for the end of battle, for their return to the haven of home.

Some will never return. Embrace these, Father, and receive them, Thy heroic servants, into Thy kingdom.

And for us at home— fathers, mothers, children, wives, sisters, and brothers of brave men overseas— whose thoughts and prayers are ever with them—help us, Almighty God, to rededicate ourselves in renewed faith in Thee in this hour of great sacrifice.

Many people have urged that I call the Nation into a single day of special prayer. But because the road is long and the desire is great, I ask that our people devote themselves in a continuance of prayer. As we rise to each new day, and again when each day is spent, let words of prayer be on our lips, invoking Thy help to our efforts.

Give us strength, too—strength in our daily tasks, to redouble the contributions we make in the physical and the material support of our armed forces.

And let our hearts be stout, to wait out the long travail, to bear sorrows that may come, to impart our courage unto our sons wheresoever they may be.

And, O Lord, give us Faith. Give us Faith in Thee; Faith in our sons; Faith in each other; Faith in our united crusade. Let not the keenness of our spirit ever be dulled. Let not the impacts of temporary events, of temporal matters of but fleeting moment—let not these deter us in our unconquerable purpose.

With Thy blessing, we shall prevail over the unholy forces of our enemy. Help us to conquer the apostles of greed and racial arrogancies. Lead us to the saving of our country, and with our sister Nations into a world unity that will spell a sure peace—a peace invulnerable to the schemings of unworthy

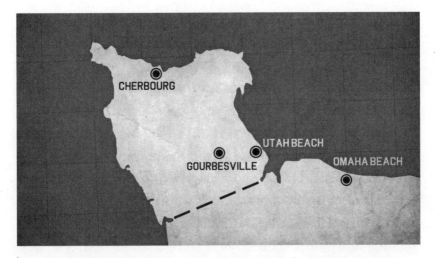

Normandy—Cherbourg. *Courtesy of Brannon Judd and Pritchett Cotten*

men. And a peace that will let all of men live in freedom, reaping the just rewards of their honest toil.

Thy will be done, Almighty God.

Amen.[2]

On the beaches of Normandy, the 4th Infantry Division assaulted Utah Beach, the D-Day landing area closest to the port of Cherbourg. They met fierce, but lighter, resistance than the hail of gunfire raining down on the 1st Infantry Division when they hit Omaha Beach to the east. Once the 4th landed on the beach, they came under both artillery and small-arms attack from German 88s and machine-gun nests. Some of the rounds hit the water near the LSTs waiting offshore. By late morning, word came from officers to the enlisted men that the 4th had secured part of the beachhead at Utah. Meanwhile at Omaha the attack was still in jeopardy. The 4th's mission was to cut across the causeway and move toward the vital port of Cherbourg. Cherbourg itself was situated on the tip of the Cotentin Peninsula.

Elements of the 90th Infantry Division arrived and began to consolidate numbers to move toward Sainte Mère Église, which was situated northwest, midway across the Cotentin Peninsula, and relieve the 82nd Airborne, whose units were fighting desperately to hold back German attempts to break through to the beaches.

As Frank's LST held off the coast, the first sergeant came to the men and said, "You boys try to get some rest. The 4th Infantry Division were the first to go in." Then taking off his helmet and wiping his brow he said, "They secured the beach. We will wait for the signal and have our turn. I expect us all to quickly be sent up with the 90th Infantry Division, because all hell will break loose when the 357th, the 358th, and 359th move past the 4th and link with airborne that survived the drops." The first sergeant put his helmet back on and walked back into the darkness of the LST's interior.

Rain and high seas were causing a delay of the invasion. The rough seas began to take their toll on the replacements, many of whom fell victim to seasickness. All were growing restless. To ease the high emotions of the moment, a captain ordered the men to perform exercises. They also rechecked each other's equipment, especially the inflatable vest. The storms and constant wave action caused Frank and Esworthy to become sick, and both began to throw up violently.

Frank looked at Esworthy and gasped, "Oh hell, my stomach ain't liking it." Not long after the ships began the journey, Frank and Esworthy had felt the first pangs of of sea sickness.

Now Esworthy patted Harold's shoulder while watching him throw up yet again and said, "I'll just be glad to get off this damn boat!" Finally, as darkness fell, the sea sickness abated. The two men sat down beside the third tank from the opening, sleeping soundly till near dawn.

Around June 12, before daylight, PFC Frank awoke suddenly hearing his mother shouting, "Harold!" He looked up and saw dark images and the sound of what appeared to be planes, distant explosions, and flashes of light across the sky. It was like awakening into a nightmare. Frank turned and saw soldiers praying and others puking from nervousness and sea sickness. Frank closed his eyes, thinking of home with a smile and with a low mumble said, "Momma's praying," before he dozed back off to sleep.

The blast of gunfire from destroyers close by jarred Frank from his nap. Jumping up and gazing across the horizon and the English Channel he saw an armada of Allied ships. The smoke and noise from destroyer guns combined with flashes in the early daylight of rocket fire. Looking toward Utah Beach, everyone watched as the LST neared the shore.

As the LST approached the beach, the first sergeant hollered to the men to prepare themselves. He came over to Frank and Esworthy and said, "Got that BAR ready?"

"Yes, Sergeant! She's ready for action," replied Frank.

"Good. We're to reinforce and support the initial invasion. We'll move off the beach to a holding point. Then await orders to move up to where the 90th Infantry is fighting. The 4th Infantry led the assault on the Krauts at Utah Beach, and the 90th arrived on Utah just behind the 4th. That is who we will be replacing. First, we will dig in and wait for the rest to unload. The Merderet Bridge is the key. Hope the 82nd can hold it till we all get there."

Looking at the company, the first sergeant told the soldiers, "Double-check your weapons and rest up."

"Yes, Sergeant," Frank replied.

He looked at Esworthy and said, "I've torn this BAR apart enough. She's ready but I'm going to take that damned tripod off because it keeps the gun too high off the ground."

Esworthy said, "Less weight too." He sighed. "This means we're on this damned boat even longer."

Throughout the dawns early light the two watched and heard the roar of planes assisting the airborne units and seaborn infantry assaults. As daybreak continued across Normandy PFC Frank witnessed a fortress of ships as far as one could see and the sounds of combat erupting in all directions.

Frank looked as if in a dream as one of the Sherman tank soldiers pointed towards the cliffs of Pointe Du Hoc and said, "The Krauts will be waiting on us as we move into the peninsula."

Around 1300 the LST carrying Frank and many fellow replacements received the signal to unload on Utah Beach. Frank looked at Paul Esworthy and said, "Time to get off this boat!"

"Amen to that!" responded Esworthy.

The door opened, and the first tank rolled off before disappearing beneath the water. The tank and crew mercifully drowned. The LST's door closed, and the craft maneuvered to a different position, causing the men to grab the sides and each other to keep from falling. The boat turned and circled back to find a better spot to unload. Finally, the door reopened, and the men in the infantry unloaded into chest-deep water. Afterwards the tanks unloaded. German and Allied artillery and distant machine-gun fire could be heard from the Utah Beach area. This was the last beach area before the village of Pointe Du Hoc to its west. The group was ordered to dig in. After dark the men began guard duty, two men to a hole. One would sleep while the other watched, rotating until morning. They had been assembled as reserves for the 90th Infantry Division.

All unnecessary gear was to be discarded. PFCs Frank and Esworthy discarded their gas masks. While they worked together digging their foxhole, PFC Frank had stated, "If something happens, don't keep a bipod on the BAR! The rifle is already well balanced, and the kick don't matter much." He discarded the bipod along with his gas mask.

Harold had found during training with Esworthy that of the two he was the better foxhole digger, so he carried the entrenchment shovel. Esworthy carried a pick. Esworthy broke up the soil and Frank would shovel it out. At midnight June 14, Frank and Esworthy were told to expect to join combat units in the morrow.

90th Division at Utah Beach

On June 10, 1944, the 90th Infantry had received orders to attack across Turqueville-Reuville-Audouville-la-Hubert to the Merderet River and relieve the 82nd Airborne. Fighting had become vicious as the division moved by Sainte Mère Église near the river. Elements of the 357th Infantry arrived at the La Fière Causeway and joined with soldiers of the 82nd Airborne to secure the area. Afterwards, the 90th Infantry began moving towards Gourbesville. Rendezvous points near Picauville had been set up, and casualties occurred every step of the way. To take objectives near Gourbesville required an immediate resort to replacements and resupply.

At daylight on June 15, a sergeant arrived and yelled, "Okay, Shit-for-the-birds, roll up your flaps! Snap your cap! Gather around, we're moving out from this JANFU!" Frank and Esworthy, already near the first sergeant, stood up as others gathered. The sergeant continued, "You men have been assigned to the 2nd Battalion of the 357th Infantry, Company G." The sergeant called out a list of names including PFC Frank and Esworthy and said, "If I called your name, fall out and gather around." He continued, "Take a knee. The 357th has been ordered to take Gourbesville. We will load up on trucks and travel across the Merderet River at the La Fière Bridge. Then near Picauville we will move by foot to your unit. You will meet up with survivors of the 82nd Airborne and the 325th GIR [Glider Infantry Regiment] that linked with our regiment." He paused. Then in a stern tone he looked at the replacements and said, "There won't be any resting! We'll move across the Cotentin to cut off any Krauts from getting in or out!"

Gazing at the men and catching the eyes of Frank, the sergeant said, "What's your name, PFC?"

"Frank," he responded.

"Good, are you a damn good shot with that Bad Ass Rifle?"

"Hell, yes! Best in the 271st!" Frank shouted back.

"Well PFC, lead us out with that Bad Ass Rifle! Only seventeen of the men that I came in with are still with us." Then, he looked at another squad with engineers and yelled, "Keep the Bangalore torpedoes ready. We'll need them to cut through barbed wire!"

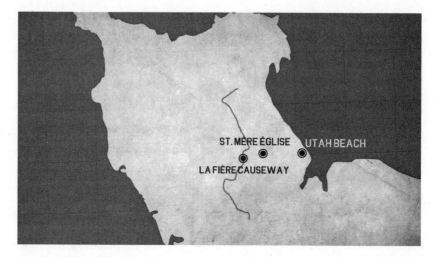

Normandy—La Fière Causeway. *Courtesy of Brannon Judd and Pritchett Cotten*

Esworthy looked at Harold and said, "We need to get out of the infantry."

Harold just shook his head and replied, "Oh, Lordy, what have we got ourselves into?"

Soon the replacements linked with elements of the 357th Infantry and together spread out from a crossroad near Écoquenéauville not far from the La Fière Causeway.

In combat Frank carried ten magazines loaded with twenty rounds each. The BAR was a .30–06-caliber weapon. It was the main machine gun used in U.S. infantry rifle squads. The BAR's larger size and lethal potential drew immediate attention from German snipers and forward observers. Frank also carried a 1911 .45-caliber pistol along with four magazines holding seven rounds each. He relied on the BAR or M1 because he couldn't shoot as well with the .45. Beyond the guns, Frank kept at least six hand grenades attached to his chest web gear. He also carried a bayonet for an M1, which was useless to a BAR because it couldn't be attached. Instead, PFC Frank learned to train with it to locate German land mines. The length of the bayonet proved effective. Frank utilized the Case double-edged hunting knife as a last measure for personal defense. His assistant gunner, PFC Paul Esworthy, carried ten magazines for the BAR, plus his own magazines for the M1 Grand.

Company G, 2nd Battalion of the 357th Infantry moved toward the town of Gourbesville. The sounds of war, including that of small arms and mortar rounds, got louder as the men eased forward. Frank was at the front of his squad along with Esworthy. Trailing behind him was another soldier who carried a World War I-era Springfield with an attached grenade launcher. It was held in the same manner as a mortar gun, and when fired by a blank, it kicked severely but did its job of launching a grenade. The remaining riflemen in the squad trailed behind, staying thirty to forty feet from each other. The same arrangement was in place from company to company as the 357th cautiously moved up the peninsula. Frank could see the intense effects of war everywhere: dead cattle, scattered debris, bodies of soldiers, and the smell of war. Moving cautiously, Company G spread out away from the beach across the green fields and toward the sound of shelling and small arms fire.

90th Division fighting for Gourbesville

As they neared Gourbesville, the company came under defi-
lade fire that included two German machine-gun nests armed
with MG-42s. These were commonly called "Hitler's Buzz Saw."

A sergeant shouted, "Frank, find cover and give covering
fire. Take out the MGs!"

Frank rolled into a bomb crater, then crawled up the hill and
located the first German machine-gun nest. He ran through
three magazines wiping it out. Pausing just for a moment, he
realized he had killed his first human beings. Then with a quick
turn, he gained a good position to fire upon another machine-gun
nest. Hearing the sergeant curse, Harold looked back with some

confusion and focused on the sergeant yelling at him. The sound of combat combined with adrenaline created confusion.

Frank heard the sergeant repeat, "Now! Frank! Damn it! Move, damn it!"

Harold grabbed his assistant gunner and ran thirty yards. They hit the ground and rolled into another crater just as a German 88 blasted the crater he had recently vacated. Frank realized that the sergeant had seen combat before and must have known the ground they had just occupied had been immediately zeroed in for attack by German mortar and artillery fire. A BAR drew attention. Desperate fighting continued as Frank and Esworthy shot down four German defenders attempting to fall back. Combat was surreal. The sounds, smells, and adrenaline combined with continuing, acute concentration as Frank moved forward with his BAR.

Frank realized from the loss of other BAR riflemen that German forward observers were training artillery specifically onto BAR positions. Frank worked on the trigger pull to make it as sensitive as possible so that three rounds fired at a touch of the trigger. The saltwater and sand slowed the action, so Frank took that opportunity to clean the three gas ports and the trigger assembly by applying light oil. Then he went back into action. The training at Camp Shelby and years of hunting with Uncle Pharris made cleaning his gun a quick operation for Frank. It was also instinctive to Frank to conserve the rounds, which served not only to improve accuracy, but also helped to delay Germans from locating his BAR. This process worked during the day, but as night fell Harold knew the fire suppressor on the end of the barrel would do little to conceal the BAR.

He told Esworthy, "Firing at night, it resembles more of a flame thrower." At nightfall Frank began to switch back and forth between the BAR and the M1 to avoid detection. It became a very effective technique. Improvise, overcome, and adapt—these were the essential elements of survival. Frank's entire upbringing had made him a superb fighter.

Late morning on June 16, Company G moved cautiously onward. Gazing across the landscape, Frank noticed a scene that would be all too common across Normandy—trees covered with parachutes blowing back and forth in the wind. Esworthy motioned to Frank to look below the chutes. Frank and others in the 357th saw countless soldiers of the 82nd hanging limp and mangled, missing limbs and riddled with bullets, while helplessly caught in the trees. These were the airborne soldiers dropped previously and tasked with fighting both retreating German beach defenders and, more importantly, holding off German reinforcements rushing to counterattack the invading Allied force. The soldiers hanging dead in the trees had found their mission cut short in the cruelest manner. Yet many of the 82nd had survived the drop and set about their task as best they could with diminished numbers.

The 357th deployed and linked with the remnants of the 325th Glider Infantry Regiment. In the distance, German grenadiers reinforced with tanks attempted to dislodge the concentration of U.S. infantry. The movement of the 357th was temporary halted by a massive artillery barrage that pinned most of the regiment. Afterwards, the line of U.S. soldiers moved forward. Many elements, including Frank's, linked with 82nd Airborne survivors. PFC Frank and Esworthy gazed over a small hedgerow and located the outskirts of the town. Word was passed along the line to prepare to defend. Frank heard the distant thunder of Sherman tanks moving up from Utah Beach. In the meantime, some of the men they'd linked with in the 82nd helped PFC Frank figure out how to put on one of their parachute-style helmets in order to add more camouflage to his position as BAR gunner. Ahead lay the hedgerow of the town of Gourbesville. PFC Frank looked at Esworthy and said, "We've made it to our destination!"

At Gourbesville, a large barrage of U.S. artillery, mostly coordinated by naval ships, attacked German positions. The 357th, along with the Glider Infantry and 82nd Airborne remnants, sprang forward. The German defenders recovering from the barrage began firing from their positions. Running crater to crater, Frank and Esworthy rolled and returned fire. Several times the German defenders withdrew only to receive reinforcements and counterattack. This led to desperate hand-to-hand combat along with exchanges of hand grenades. The importance of the town caused the fighting to continue long into the night. In one day of fighting, the 357th suffered ninety-nine killed in action (KIA). On June 16 and into the pre-dawn of June 17, U.S. infantry crossed and secured parts of the hedgerow outside Gourbesville. They had maneuvered around the towns of

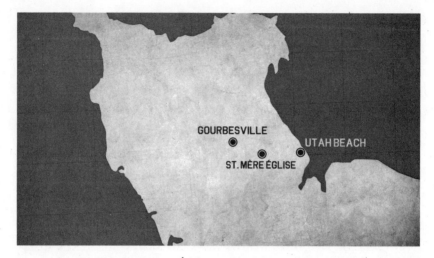

Normandy—Sainte Mère Église. *Courtesy of Brannon Judd and Pritchett Cotten*

Amfreville and their principal goal of Gourbesville. Frank and Esworthy didn't recognize most of the men around them, as most were replacements, but the horror of war was just beginning.

Since they moved from their positions along Utah Beach, the USS *Texas* had provided fire support because no ground artillery could yet be brought in. PFC Frank could occasionally see rounds fly overhead, and their explosions put him on the ground. Then he and the others would move forward, using the craters for cover. After securing the causeway and the bridge over the Merderet River, the Allied fire support dwindled. Frank and Esworthy worked as a team true to the infantry motto, "shoot, move, and communicate." Approaching a tree line, the men of

Company G continued to see airborne parachutes. The 357th with artillery support made it through a maze of hedgerows near Amfreville. There they found the Germans soldiers had built bunkers with railroad ties covered with five feet of dirt; these bunkers were very difficult to assault. To Frank's shock, on several occasions French women emerged from the German bunkers and fired at him. Frank and Esworthy assaulted one bunker where German soldiers attempted to flee. Frank killed them with just two taps of the BAR. Suddenly two girls ran out of the same bunker. They carried German rifles and turned to fire on Frank and Esworthy, who immediately fired back, killing them both. Frank and Esworthy jumped into a crater and reloaded while looking at each other in disbelief.

"What the hell was that?" Esworthy yelled.

"I don't know but they'll kill us just as much as the damn Nazis!" Frank shouted back.

Moving closer to the hedgerows, the 357th Infantry managed to advance. On several more occasions, women were found to be helping the German Army. Once the bullets flew, combat took control, and the 357th crept through the hedgerows while German snipers and forward observers continued to target BAR positions.

The next morning PFC Frank and PFC Esworthy moved forward, immediately engaging the enemy and digging foxholes each time they were forced to stop. Artillery fire from 155mm howitzers gave some support against a group of German tanks that tested the flanks of the 357th. Bangalore torpedoes were

Hedgerow fighting—a soldier with the 357th Infantry of the 90th Division preparing to fire a grenade

very effective at opening the German barbed wire, but there was another method of advance. One soldier would lay over the barbed wire, and the others would step one boot on the small of his back and go beyond to fire on Germans. The BAR riflemen were usually first over to clear out German resistance.

Some wire was too difficult to cross in this manner, and that's where the Bangalore torpedoes came in. For instance, a one-point wire was too wide and couldn't be cut. A dedicated unit had to put together the Bangalore torpedoes so a tech sergeant could fire them. This would cut the wire like a hacksaw.

As the men continued the struggle to take Gourbesville, they were near exhaustion and were given some rest. During the night, word arrived that to increase aggressiveness the 90th Infantry Division commander had been replaced by General Eugene M. Landrum. At dawn a massive artillery barrage occurred, signaling the next attack. Frank heard German artillery rounds. In most cases, these passed over him.

Harold looked at Paul and repeated, "The one that hits you, you ain't gonna hear."

The lines moved slightly, and gaps were consolidated for a larger attack that evening. The goal was to take Gourbesville. PFC Frank's survivability skills and expertise with the BAR had by then been noticed by many, including his platoon sergeant. As a result he and Esworthy were placed on night patrols to make contact with other companies and guard gaps in the line.

The 357th attacked German units holding the high ground. Then they turned and pressed on to attack Gourbesville. In heavy fighting the 357th pushed German soldiers into more hedgerows and slowly pressed the enemy into Gourbesville. Elements of the 1st and 2nd Battalions entered parts of the town and moved to gain the high ground.

On June 18, beginning at 0500, the assault of the city began again, but the 357th was thrown back. The 357th attacked in desperate fighting throughout the rest of the day. In an effort to relieve pressure, the 358th Infantry Regiment worked on the flank and captured some of the high ground. The 359th conducted patrols as PFC Frank and the men of the 357th dug in and held

90th Division in desperate hedgerow fighting

their positions in the center. Before beginning their next night patrol, Frank and Esworthy cleaned their weapons, taking turns with one on watch while the other meticulously cleaned the sooty pieces and the gas port on the BAR. At dawn on June 19, Company G moved to another location near the town where an assault on a heavily defended part of the hedgerows was required. Artillery fired smoke to give the men cover, but the returning machine-gun fire and word of further German reinforcements stopped the attack. Instead, the 357th was ordered to hold the position. Throughout the day they received more replacements to support the assault. By evening German artillery destroyed every tree between the lines. PFC Frank looked over the debris-covered field; it was littered with shattered trees, fencing, and a formerly beautiful farm, while cattle lay dead or writhing in pain. From their foxhole, both Frank and Esworthy said, "This is FUBAR." War left a permanent impression upon the mind and senses.

Both sides continually exchanged artillery attacks, causing causalities to mount. One round from a German 88 scored a direct hit upon a foxhole to Frank and Esworthy's right. The blast and concussion showered dirt and debris everywhere, and nothing remained of the men in the foxhole. Before daylight Harold awoke again to his mother's voice saying, "Harold." He smiled and said, "Mom's praying again." The regiment moved into a flanking maneuver away from their dug-in positions.

On June 20 Frank and Esworthy moved forward with the platoon and elements of the 82nd Airborne that joined the 2nd Battalion moving further around Gourbesville. The orders were to seize the railroad heading from Gourbesville to Beauval. Many of the airborne soldiers were carrying the Thompson machine gun, and many littered the field. Harold Frank would never forget what he had seen along the countryside. So many 82nd and 101st Airborne had been killed in action, helplessly slaughtered in the vulnerable window of descent and landing. The memory of them still hanging in trees with their parachutes and bullet-ridden bodies in crashed gliders would remain with Frank the rest of his life.

90th Division meeting up with the 82nd Airborne during a lull in fighting to save the Merderet Bridge

While considering the parachute snags in the trees and the ground littered with gliders, PFC Frank met a soldier with the 82nd and exclaimed, "You boys were scattered all over creation!"

The airborne soldier, also a PFC, replied, "Yeah, it was a SNAFU. They dumped us out and we missed our drop zones—which may have been a good thing. The damn Krauts didn't figure out our numbers or locations."

With a sigh he looked down at a dead German soldier, then up at a dead airborne soldier hanging by a chute and said, "Several of our airborne had been shot to pieces while parachuting, and later the same happened to those caught hanging by their chutes in the trees."

Other men in the 357th, many recent replacements, took the advantage of picking up the helmets of the airborne soldiers and quickly adopted the web netting used on airborne helmets. It would prove effective for concealment. They cut the camo parachutes and tucked them around the steel pot and into the liner to keep them tight. This prevented the metal helmet from glinting in the light. The men also put all manner of items in the cargo webbing to help them blend into their surroundings.

Together the mixed group of U.S. soldiers dug in as more fighting erupted. This was directed towards forward elements of the 82nd Airborne and the 90th Infantry. Heavy fighting ensued, and parts of these units had to fall back into the city. About midnight, the 357th, along with elements of the 82nd Airborne, regained complete control of Gourbesville and adjacent areas. Knowing that German counterattacks to reopen contact with Cherbourg would continue, PFC Frank and the surviving veterans of the 357th moved to better locations. Expecting a German attack at any time, Company G noticed good defensive ground behind a French farmhouse. The platoon sergeant ordered Frank to set up the heavy, water-cooled, .30-caliber machine gun behind the farmhouse, where there was a good field of view toward the German forces gathered along a distant line of trees. A well was located and immediately utilized to refill canteens. Before filling, the soldiers tossed water filtration tablets in the water, causing the farmer, who was still at his farm, to become upset. It turned out he believed the soldiers had poisoned his water. After pulling the water out, each soldier took a drink. The farmer realized his water was safe, only to then observe the machine-gun firing position.

A hog was tied up in the line of fire. The sergeant ordered the farmer to untie the hog and move it to another location. The soldiers dug into position, but the farmer refused to remove the hog. The sergeant had to untie the hog, move it, and retie it away from the machine-gun firing position. The farmer ran out, untied the hog and moved it back, blocking the firing position. The sergeant tried to explain the urgency and danger of attack to the farmer and moved the hog again. After a few minutes the farmer returned with the hog, causing the first sergeant to pull out his 1911 .45-caliber pistol and shoot the hog. The farmer sat down by the hog and wept.

The whole event bothered Harold, who looked at Paul Esworthy and said, "What a waste. The man must be crazy."

Esworthy looked and replied, "Why would you tie a hog right between the lines?"

"FUBAR," both replied.

By June 19, in total, since pushing out from Utah Beach and securing the bridge over the Merderet River, the 357th suffered 783 casualties.

CHAPTER 11

Holding the Peninsula: "Yeah, It Doesn't Burn as Bad Now"

T he men of the 357th dug in with foxholes twenty feet apart and two soldiers per hole. They had to stop German attempts to get in or out of the area and, most importantly, prevent them from breaking through to retake the port of Cherbourg, which was crucial to the continuing Allied invasion. The remnants of the 357th, 358th, and 359th regiments prepared defensive positions to hold out until reinforcement from the 79th Infantry Division arrived. The regiment near Gourbesville had been decimated, suffering 730 casualties including its commanding officer and many NCOs (noncommissioned officers). By June 21, 1944, the 357th expected a major counterattack, and several company NCOs came from regimental headquarters. They warned the men to be prepared for a major attack. Later that morning PFC Frank was given permission to attend a short sermon from the Army chaplain.

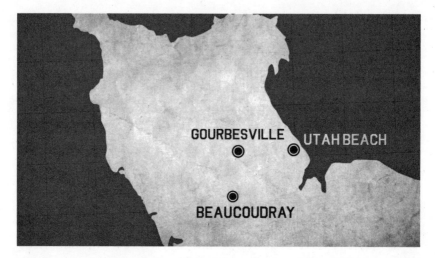

Normandy—Beaucoudray and Gourbesville. *Courtesy of Brannon Judd and Pritchett Cotten*

Afterwards, training quickly began in preparation for a major German counterattack with tanks. Civilians working with the French Resistance reported the German advance was imminent and sent night patrols to probe German positions. On many occasions they ran into German patrols doing the same, leading to deadly hand-to-hand encounters. PFC Frank and PFC Esworthy were dug in beside a small building adjacent to the hard service road. A German soldier rose thirty yards away, and PFC Frank shot him with the BAR. Immediately German artillery shelled the small building, causing it to collapse. The rumble of German tanks increased, and German infantry began to move forward.

In the excitement a U.S. Army officer, a second lieutenant from the 357th, fell beside Frank and Esworthy and said, "Let me hit one."

Frank said, "Help yourself, there are plenty to go around."

A German soldier stood up on a hedgerow and shouted the name "Ludwig," right as Frank put three rounds through him. Immediately, Frank heard a German tank coming up the road. German Artillery opened up, and a round hit a farm building just a few feet from the position of Frank and Esworthy. The blast took out the roof. It had no doubt been meant to silence the BAR. A replacement that Frank didn't know was shot near the front of the helmet. It pierced the metal and went around the liner and back out the steel on the opposite side. Miraculously, it never hit the soldier's scalp, but it did give him a headache. Together, Frank, Esworthy, and the lieutenant fired on the German soldiers until the Panzer tanks came into sight. Then they fell back near a radio operator. While given covering fire, the radio operator directed artillery fire, knocking out two tanks and forcing the remaining tanks and infantry support to retreat. The remaining elements of the 357th fell back a hundred yards to a strong defensive position near a hedgerow they had captured. They held the position the rest of the day, and the Germans didn't attack again. The men with PFC Frank and the 357th were ordered to dig in around the road intersection and hedgerow. Their orders remained the same: stop any German units attempting to head to, or retreat from, Cherbourg.

Beaucoudray in July 1944—357th soldiers resting

Just after daylight on June 22, 1944, PFC Frank was on a patrol and entered a small castle complete with a moat. He went room to room to clear the structure. All was empty but one room that looked like an office. As Harold and three others entered, they looked at a German Regular Army colonel still at his desk doing paperwork. They ordered him to surrender.

He replied in perfect English, "I will not surrender to anyone below my rank."

The patrol sergeant walked into the room and hit him in the head, knocking his hat off. He immediately ordered the officer to surrender.

The sergeant looked at him and said, "You're nothing but a 'gold brick.'"

Then motioning to the squad, the sergeant said, "Get this Kraut out of here."

The patrol transferred the German POW to an Army intelligence officer, and the squad returned to their firing positions. German artillery, particularly 88s, opened on the 357th late that evening and through the day. Frank remembered how the quiet erupted, replaced by an earth-shaking boom and rattle that jarred every bone and tooth. This was the prelude to a large-scale German counterattack with tanks. A wide assortment of tanks, including Tigers, came in, all without infantry support. The fighting to hold Gourbesville became desperate, and only coordinated artillery attacks pushed back the tanks. At one point shrapnel fell on PFC Frank's assistant gunner, Esworthy, who yelled to Frank, "Harold, I'm hit and burning."

Harold crawled over and knocked debris away. It included a red-hot piece of shrapnel one inch long. Frank tapped Esworthy and smiled, asking "Is that better?"

Paul replied, "Yeah, it doesn't burn as bad now."

That night the lines held. The sweat of the day caused the men to shake with chills throughout the night.

For many unaccustomed to intensive combat, the reality in each rifle squad and infantry company is very different than "after-action reports" may indicate. The casualty rates for the 357th were high, and replacements came in, which made remembering names very difficult. All stripes and rank insignias had

Beaucoudray hedgerow nicknamed "Death Valley" by the 357th Infantry

been torn from uniforms, aggravating the problem of forgotten names, and from time to time unit organization became extremely tangled. Although the men were in different units, squads, and companies, they would watch out for each other by filling in the weak points and heading out on patrols with men whose names they didn't know or couldn't remember. Late on June 24 and early on the twenty-fifth, civilians warned of more and larger counterattacks. Yet the regiment was waiting for reinforcement from the 79th Infantry and had been ordered to conserve what ammo they had and only fire if fired upon.

During the night on June 25, Paul Esworthy and Harold Frank tried to sleep. Frank was chilled from the sweat of the day, and the cold of the night made it difficult to stay warm. Esworthy noticed his restlessness and said, "You okay?"

"Yeah, just can't get warm, but I'll be all right."

Frank began to doze off and, finally, to sleep. Esworthy was just about to wake Frank to take guard when Frank jumped awake. Frank, looking startled, turned to Esworthy, who asked, "Is your mom praying again?"

"Sounded like she was right here," replied Harold.

Soon German artillery erupted and the expected attack began. German soldiers attacked across the front and flanks, resorting to hand grenades and hand-to-hand combat. The attack was so close that a U.S. Army sergeant from another company a few yards from Harold prepared to fire a bazooka on a German panzer but then diverted to fire point blank into a German soldier, blowing the German in half. The fighting continued until daybreak when the German attack quietened down. The remnants of the 357th along with airborne troops captured forty German soldiers. PFC Frank noted at least a dozen of the 357th had been killed. Thinking the attack was over at daybreak on the twenty-sixth, Frank and Esworthy sat on the ground above their foxhole eating C-rations for breakfast. Dirt suddenly flew up, and then the two heard the report of a rifle. The two fell back into their foxhole and tried to look up to determine where the shots came from. The platoon sergeant and several in the squad yelled from forty feet away, "Stay down, the Kraut sees you! We'll get him." Fire erupted and the platoon sergeant and two others sighted in on one tree eighty yards to the front. They shot into the foliage. One German soldier flopped down, still partially hanging in the tree. Upon inspection the German had climbed up the tree with his Mauser, tying himself to the tree to avoid falling, but he now hung dead from the same rope. The U.S. infantry fought for each other, becoming a band of brothers. They hadn't slept much for several days and needed equipment checks and cleaning. The first sergeant arrived and told Frank and Esworthy that the real fight was to cut off the last remaining route supplying German forces in the Cotentin Peninsula, especially Cherbourg. The desperate attempt to keep the remaining supply line open to German forces in Cherbourg had begun a few days earlier on June 19 with the 357th relieving elements of the 90th U.S. Infantry. In desperation to gain control of the last hardtop road, the first sergeant carefully ordered each platoon in Company G to spread out, with BAR riflemen leading. Heavy fighting erupted at Frank and Esworthy's front. One German machine-gun nest after another was wiped out by Frank's BAR as armored German halftracks arrived to reinforce. German infantry came out, but one halftrack was disabled, and all the Germans were killed by BAR fire. All day long German patrols and armor attempted to dislodge the 357th to the point that hand-grenade exchanges and hand-to-hand combat intensified. Through the night and into the morning, the lines were improved and reinforcements consisting mostly of replacements dug in around what was left of Company G.

Suddenly a German panzer ripped right through the center of the company. PFC Frank and PFC Esworthy ignored the panzer and gunned down the German infantry support. They were joined by BAR fire opposite the tank to create a deadly crossfire. The tank opened up with machine-gun fire to silence the BAR fire and moved closer towards Frank's position. The shaking of the ground rattled every bone in the body, and the two prepared to find a better position while U.S. artillery support roared overhead with rounds coming in within fifty yards. The shelling lasted for several minutes. Frank noticed the that the tank was on fire, and they were ordered to attack. With the remnants of three platoons, the 357th wiped out pockets of German infantry still fighting along the road.

As more tanks arrived, Frank and Esworthy carefully moved into another area of hedgerows. Looking into the trees, on several occasions they spotted and shot snipers. Slowly, a Sherman tank moved up on their left flank, thirty yards from their position.

Esworthy looked at Frank and said, "That's what we need to be in."

The tank moved up the five-foot bank, and suddenly an 88 round shook the tank. The turret blew off, and several soldiers who were completely on fire fell out and died.

"I think I'll stay in the infantry," Frank said.

Watching in horror, Esworthy replied, "Yeah, me too."

Fighting slowed down by late June 1944, and they were ordered to dig in. After finishing their defensive positions, the men filled up on ammo, cleaned weapons, and waited until

German tank destroyed during the 90th Infantry Division's fighting in the Cotentin Peninsula

dawn to reengage. Much of the Cotentin Peninsula was littered with Holstein milk cows and various horses killed from the war. PFC Frank and PFC Esworthy left their foxhole and sat next to one of the dead animals for protection while eating K-rations. They were now hardened veterans and had learned to be mindful of every building, tree, and ridgeline. In addition, they had to be careful when noticing abandoned weapons. The Germans would booby trap the bodies of U.S. soldiers and purposely place explosives that were triggered by the picking up discarded German Lugers—guns U.S. soldiers sought for their own defense. By the end of June, the company was ordered to move to another location. Finally, they were secure enough for the men to get needed rest.

June 27 and twenty-eighth the remnants of the 357th combined with other companies and filled slots in other companies to repair defensive positions. On the twenty-eighth, word came that relief was heading to the 357th from leading elements of the 79th Infantry. Upon arrival, elements of the 357th began to fall back to receive hot showers and badly-needed new uniforms, boots, and ammo. Company G of the 357th finally hit the showers on Independence Day. Company G was down to approximately twenty men, many of whom were replacements. Frank and Esworthy never knew their names. Regardless, they made their way to the rear to rest. While en route they paused by a railroad track so PFC Frank and PFC Esworthy could stop and assist MPs in rounding up seventeen German soldiers who were bearing a white flag and surrendering.

Later, the men of Company G changed into new uniforms. Harold also enjoyed a new pair of boots. They reloaded with the ammo and cigarettes, which were freely distributed, but Harold rarely smoked. He knew Annie and Pap wouldn't approve. Exhaustion and fatigue finally caught up with PFC Frank and PFC Esworthy. They rested and cleaned their weapons. Frank even managed to write three letters home. The morning of July 5 began with Frank hearing his mom speaking in another dream. Over a hot breakfast, Harold looked at Esworthy and said, "Annie woke me again."

"Oh damn...all hell is about to break loose!"

The two looked around and saw many more new replacements and others they didn't recognize. A sergeant appeared out of nowhere and ordered the group to gather around.

"I'm looking for Frank and Esworthy," he said.

Frank looked up and said, "You found us."

The sergeant replied, "The Germans appear to be massing for another attack to hit our positions during the night. We've lost contact with two companies. You're our most experienced BAR riflemen, and we need your help. Saddle up, we're heading back."

They returned to the front and passed through a village with a sign, 'ST Mary,' and continued toward Beaucoudray. They moved into a field with a good view of the front alongside a hedgerow. They were ordered to dig in. By noon they were dug in and prepared for attack. A new replacement came out of his foxhole and pointed at a Nazi Luger sitting on top of the remnants of a wooden bunker.

Frank yelled out, "Hey buddy! Don't go for that Luger."

He looked back at Frank and asked, "Why? You trying to get it too?"

Frank picked up his BAR and aimed at the Luger, causing the replacement to take cover. Frank fired one round. Immediately the bunker exploded from the booby-trapped gun. The young replacement jumped back into his foxhole shaking from the experience. He yelled back as the dust settled, "Lord God, it would've killed me."

CHAPTER 12

"Now We're Going to See What Tough Really Is!"

Near dark on July 6, 1944, the sergeant approached PFC Frank and Esworthy's foxhole and said, "I've formed a ten-man patrol to contact I and L Companies who have been cut off. You two are our experienced BAR gunners. Engineers will go with you to establish communication. A sergeant from L Company will lead the patrol, get ready."

After the sergeant left, PFC Frank looked at PFC Esworthy and said, "We may not make it back from this patrol."

Esworthy nodded in agreement as he looked into the darkness and said, "You've taught me a lot. I'll stay back in the patrol and maybe we'll make it. Hell, we've made it this far."

Frank looked at the BAR and said, "As long as I have ammo, we have a chance, but all these replacements are undertrained. Some have never held a weapon before the war."

"You got that right!" replied Esworthy.

Beaucoudray foxholes

Frank added quickly, "If something happens to me, find someone you can train." Shaking his head and making a quick laugh, Frank looked toward the stars and said, "Oh, Lordy, A country boy will find a way to survive. Let's eat our C-rats. Looks like beef hash."

"It's not like home, that's for damn sure!" Esworthy replied.

After midnight the patrol moved out, and PFC Frank with his BAR was near the front and PFC Esworthy near the rear. Each soldier was approximately thirty feet apart from the others. One of the replacements saw movement and attempted to shoot, but the M1 misfired. The sergeant leading the patrol grabbed the rifle, which was dirty, and told the private to clean it imme-diately. He told him not to waste water, but to piss the dirt off, which the solider did. Harold shook his head and remembered what Edward and Uncle Pharris had taught him: "If you know the equipment and keep it clean, it'll take care of you." Looking at his BAR and then at the replacement's weapon, he wondered how a soldier could leave any weapon so dirty when survival depended on it.

Quietly, the ten-man patrol continued into the night. Rain moved in as the patrol neared a hedgerow. At one point Frank's feet stumbled in a hedgerow. He fell on a German soldier, whom he stabbed instantly with his Case hunting knife—only to find the man was already dead.

As the patrol was searching for I and L Companies, elements of the 357th received reinforcements and moved forward to close in on the village of Beaucoudray. The Germans launched a mas-sive offensive at the same time. It consisted of three battalions led by the elite 15th German Parachute Regiment, which had reinforced the German lines the day before. The attacked pushed much of the 357th back from the town, leaving some companies cut off and other elements intermingled. The patrol trying to find I and L Companies was unaware of the desperate situation they had entered. They were well behind German lines.

Several attempts were made by the 90th Division to reestab-lish contact with remnants of the 357th around Beaucoudray. All failed. Every effort was hurled back with heavy losses. Most of the officers and noncoms were killed in the fighting. On the evening of the seventh, the Allied lines had been nearly overrun. The fighting stiffened on the right flank. Now the 79th Infantry and 82nd Airborne Divisions fought to hold their own lines, thus keeping reinforcements from reaching the exposed elements of the 357th, including the now lost patrol that had been sent to find Companies I and L. The 15th German Parachute Regiment began breaking into the rear of the 90th Division, which brought every available soldier into the fight, including cooks, air defense, and supply personnel. Everyone was infantry now. Gains were made on the left flank of the 90th Division with the push of the 83rd Infantry Division that made it into the hedgerows. Still the German line continued to move forward.

At dawn on July 7, the ten-man patrol heard fighting enveloping the area. PFC Frank and the patrol continued toward the lost companies. At 0630 the patrol reached a hardtop road, and they attempted a road crossing. PFC Frank led three others. He crossed with PFC Esworthy remaining near the rear. After crossing Frank and the other three were immediately attacked by elements of the 15th German Parachute Regiment armed with machine guns. The machine-gun fire cut through the patrol. The four were now on the German side of the road. Frank and the three others lost sight of the patrol. Frank was cut off from any survivors—including his best friend and assistant gunner, Paul Esworthy. The four-man group heard Germans moving along the road. German attacks came from several directions. The group was now aware that the fighting they'd heard the previous

Annie and Edward Lee Frank, Harold Frank's parents

Harold Frank, 1942

Edward Frank and horse Zeb

Robert Pharris and his wife, Vera

Uncle Grady and Aunt Carie

PFC Harold Frank, brother Archie, and sister Naomi, just before heading to New York, 1943

Saint Luke's Lutheran Church, Tyro, North Carolina, 2019

Harold Frank's high school in Tyro, North Carolina

Tyro High School
Basketball Champions,
1942. Left to right—
Carson Swicegood,
Tommy Michael,
[First name unknown]
Williams, Roy Haywood,
Von Nance, Harold
Frank, Douglas Parnell,
Gail Giles, Harold
Walter, and Raymous
Hilliard

Harold Frank with Davidson County fellow draftees in Lexington. Harold is in the first row, far right.

Private Harold Frank of the 69th Division in basic training uniform, Camp Shelby, Mississippi, 1943

Private Harold Frank on home leave from Camp Shelby, Mississippi, late fall, 1943. Edward and Annie's house that Harold helped build in 1931 is in background.

Harold Frank, 271st Infantry, basic training picture, Camp Shelby, Mississippi, 1943. Harold is in the back row, eleventh from the left.

Harold Frank Is War Prisoner

Pvt. Harold Frank, brother of Mrs. Keith Lyon, 520 East Cemetery street, is a prisoner of war of Germany according to latest information received by his family from the war department.

He is the son of Mr. and Mrs. E. L. Frank of Rt. 5, Lexington. Previous report had been that he was missing in action in France and he was given this status in an official war department casualty list published this week. However, the casualty list was somewhat behind the times for the report of his changed status was made several weeks ago.

Private Frank, 19, attended Tyro schools and was employed by the North Carolina Finishing company at Yadkin when he entered service about a year and a half ago.

Harold L. Frank Missing in Action

Pfc. Harold Lee Frank, Davidson county youth who was employed by the North Carolina Finishing company before his induction, has been missing in France since July 8, the War department has notified his parents, Mr. and Mrs. E. L. Frank, Rt. 5, Lexington.

He graduated from Tyro High school in the spring of 1942 and worked for the finishing company until April, 1943, when he entered the army and went to Camp Shelby, Mass., for basic infantry training.

He was stationed for a time at Fort Meade, Md., and was transferred to England in April, 1944.

PFC. HAROLD LEE FRANK

Reported Missing In France, July 8

Pfc. Frank In Infantry, Wrote Parents On July 6

Pfc. Harold Lee Frank, U. S. Army Infantry, son of Mr. and Mrs. E. L. Frank, of Lexington, R. 5, has been reported missing in action in France since July 8, Adjutant General Ulio informed the parents by telegram, which was received Saturday morning at ten o'clock. Further information was promised as soon as any has been received.

Pvt. Frank was inducted in April 1943, took basic training at Camp Shelby, Miss., and was sent overseas in April of this year. A letter from him dated July 6 was recently received by his parents, in which he said that he was enjoying a rest period after front line fighting. He was last home on furlough some 30 days before sailing and his parents visited him at Fort George Meade, Md., just before his departure overseas.

Pvt. Frank was graduated from Tyro High school in the class of 1942

(Continued On Page Two)

POW announcement article about PFC Harold Frank in Davidson County *Dispatch* newspaper, 1944

Harold's shaving kit turned into a letter holder

NOV. 26, 1944

Dear Harold.
Jo night while thinking
of you I will write you a few lines,
hopeing you are well. we are all well
Here at home and sure would like to
see you. archie has gone to tyro as
usual to spend the eveing and awhile
tonight. well son you ask about artis cecil
a good while ago he has been wounded
and is back over here now in a hospital
and is at home for a few days. dad
saw him at the mill and talked with
him a little while he wanted to know
about you said he hadent heared from
you for a long time. so dad told him
whiat he could. wish you could see Joe
he sure is some boy now thinks he is the
boss of the House. I am sending you some of
his pictures in this letter so you can
see how he is growing. dad Joe and all the
rest said Hello. and we are all thinking

Letter from Annie to Harold, November 26, 1944

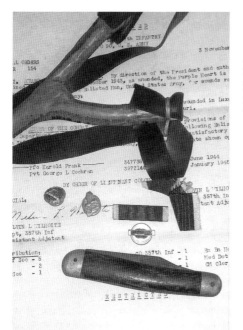

Personal wartime artifacts of PFC Harold Frank, now part of the collection of the Forks of the Yadkin and Davie County History Museum, March 7, 2016

Dresden from the perspective of the U.S. Army Air Forces VIII Bomber Command

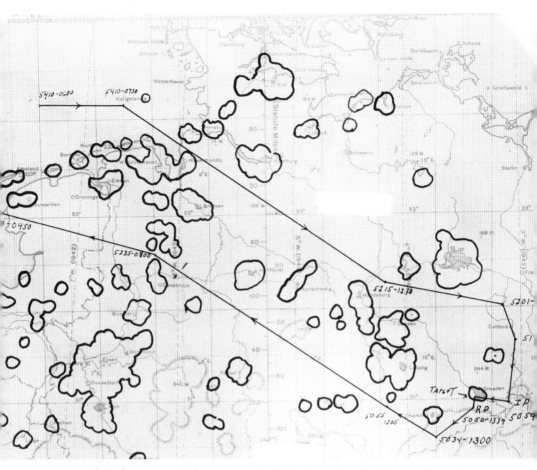

U.S. Army Air Forces VIII Bomber Command's flight plan to Dresden. IP 5059 shows the location of PFC Frank's POW camp near Klotzsche Air Field.

Harold Frank with his mother, Annie Frank, soon after returning from World War II, 1946

PFC Frank's Bible dedication page from Annie, May 3, 1943

A Sacred Token

To Harold Lee Frank.

From His Mother Mrs E. L. Frank.

May 3rd, 1943.

John Jones
Route 3,
Appleton City
Missouri
Clyde Stover
Clark Range,
Tenn.

PFC Frank's Bible with John Jones's and Clyde Stover's inscriptions written while they were POWs near Dresden

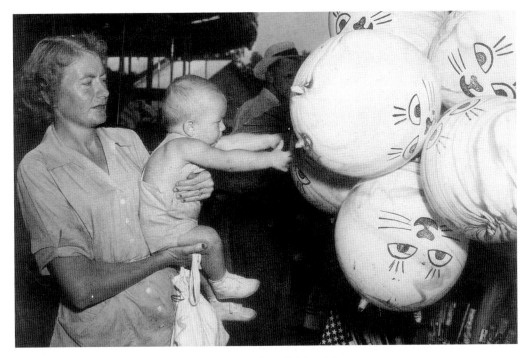

Rebe Frank, Harold Frank's wife, with their first child, Eddie, ca. 1950s

PFC Frank's Bible with POW names that Frank wrote down while in captivity

Harold Frank
at home,
looking at
a picture of
Rebe Frank

Harold Frank at a gun range firing a BAR rifle, 2017

Harold Frank's prayer of invocation before the national anthem at the Coca-Cola 600, 2017

75th Anniversary of D-Day—Harold Frank selected to lay the memorial wreath in the American Cemetery in Flanders Field

75th Anniversary of D-Day—Harold Frank walking into the Sainte Mère Église Cemetery

night was the prelude to a major German offensive. Frank found that he now led a small rifle squad.

The rifle squad continued one hundred yards while exchanging gunfire with Germans. They stumbled upon the abandoned foxholes from Companies I and L. Frank spotted an American soldier by his helmet shape and jumped in his foxhole, startling the already anxious soldier.

The man turned and Frank yelled, "I'm an American! Who are you with?"

"L Company," the soldier in the fox hole said, "the others were killed during the night, leaving the abandoned foxholes."

The rifle squad with Frank jumped into those foxholes.

It turned out that in the darkness the two companies had been overrun by German paratroopers. Some two hundred had been captured. Looking at the situation, Frank told the others, "This is a good spot. Conserve the ammo and get the Krauts as they move up the road." They heard voices of German soldiers who were completely unaware that a rifle squad still remained. The Germans walked into the ambush. Remembering lessons from Uncle Pharris on shooting quail, PFC Frank opened up as two Germans came close together. Gunfire became intense and lasted for several minutes. The Germans realized an unknown number of U.S. infantry had not been taken out. For several hours the squad hampered German reinforcements trying to break through the 90th Division. During a calm, PFC Frank called for ammo status, and each of the rifle squad said, "Getting low." Frank noticed a path in the hedgerows and rose in an

Beaucoudray Le Plessis Church near the wounding of PFC Frank

attempt to locate any others in the area. Suddenly, he felt as if he'd been kicked by a mule. He fell forward.

Frank had been shot in the shoulder by a hidden German sniper. Another in the patrol was hit in the leg, which was badly fractured. Frank and the others came under more gun fire but held. They fought off several more German attacks. Amazingly, the four fought nearly nine hours, beginning with the road crossing. They caused enough disruption to slow their portion of the German advance, and German reinforcements, including tanks, were finally deployed to handle them. The sound of the fast-approaching German tanks, combined with the knowledge that all the ammo was gone, led Frank to realize the position could no longer be held. They must leave the foxholes. Before jumping from his own foxhole, Harold lost his hunting knife, which was stained with blood from the dead German, as he grabbed his injured shoulder. The wound was bad, but Frank managed to climb out on his own. He then helped carry the soldier with the fractured leg. The four moved along the trail PFC Frank had spotted just before getting shot. It ran parallel to the hardtop and into a flooded field—which they discovered was more like a swamp. Slowing, they attempted to make their way back to Allied lines. Frank, though wounded himself, continued aiding in the carrying of the soldier with the fractured leg. They crossed the flooded ground.

Checking his badly injured shoulder, Frank said to the other injured man, "Can you help by pulling yourself up the bank?"

"I'll try," was the weak reply.

As they climbed out of the flooded field, they were greeted by a German soldier armed with a machine gun.

PFC Frank quickly removed the trigger element of his weapon and tossed it into the water, and the men surrendered. The small squad had been captured by the unit that had overrun Companies I and L. The German soldier ordered the group of four to the ground. The injured U.S. soldier with the fractured leg was immediately executed, shot through the head point blank. Harold worked to hide his own wound. The three were ordered to stand. Other Germans, all aggravated by the long fight, arrived. One officer kept yelling at the group, and none of the POWs understood the commands until rounds were fired in front of their feet. The three men stripped to show they had no hidden weapons. The guard motioned for them to redress. They marched until dark and were placed in a horse stable. Unknown to the small rifle squad, they had managed to tie up German reinforcements trying to break through Allied lines for nearly nine hours. This allowed time for the remnants of the 90th Division to restore their defenses and stabilize the lines.

For several nights they remained in barns and were joined by other captured soldiers. The German guards were Regular Army soldiers with police dogs. When the guards ordered them to march, they refused to let soldiers off the roads even when they needed to use the bathroom. Stepping off the road was certain death. PFC Frank looked at the other two soldiers and said, "Now we're going to see what tough really is!"

The War Department notified Edward and Annie Frank by telegram on Saturday, July 15, 1944, at 10:00 a.m. that PFC Harold Frank was Missing in Action (MIA). The news came as a shock as just two days earlier Annie had received a letter from Harold that was dated July 6 and said that he was doing well and had been resting from the front lines. It would be nearly four months before word arrived that Harold was alive and held as a prisoner of war. What faced Harold over the next ten months was indeed a most perilous hardship, pushing the limits of human endurance. Survival required all the training, faith, and discipline that the Great Depression and Army doggedness could muster in the young man.

CHAPTER 13

Poetic Justice

During the night of July 9, 1944, the three captured U.S. soldiers, desperate for water, managed to exchange some cigarettes for apple cider to quench their severe thirst. The following morning they were interrogated separately in a small building with a concrete floor and little furniture. A German Army captain questioned PFC Frank. He asked Frank for his name.

Harold gave his name, rank and service number and the German interrupted, "Frank? That's a German name! You're killing your own kin."

Harold replied, "Nah, Captain, my kin live near Tyro."

"Where the hell is that?" replied the German.

"Outside Lexington, North Carolina, on Highway 150, halfway between Reeds and Churchland!"

The captain noticed a Waltham pocket watch with PFC Frank, and motioned for him to hand it over. The watch belonged to

Edward, who had given it to Harold at Fort Meade, Maryland. Frank placed the watch in his hand, but as he was about to hand it over, he opened his hand and let it drop hard onto the concrete floor. The German officer yelled, "It's kaput! No good." Then he shook his head and walked away.

On July 12, the captured soldiers were placed in groups of forty to fifty American POWs. The wound in PFC Frank's shoulder continued to fester and began to ooze pus. The stench caused other POWs to move away from Frank. By July 13, he developed chills and intermittent fever. He was sure he was a goner. Harold prayed for help and once again felt the prayers of Annie shoring him up. The following day, a new POW was placed with the group. He was a U.S. Army medic. He possessed his medical kit, which the Germans had allowed him to keep. As the medic walked over to PFC Frank, Harold gazed up at the medic and said, "The good Lord is watching over me." The medic put sulfa powder and a few other medicines on the shoulder wound. After a few days, the wound healed but the bullet remained. The medic fixed the wound, saving Frank's life, but the bullet could not be extracted from the bone.

By July 16, the POWs were marched to a series of buildings adjacent to a railroad and placed in buildings. The buildings were three stories tall with bunk beds of wooden slats covered with straw. The rooms were wide open, holding around two hundred POWs in each building. The next day around 1:00 p.m., U.S. Army P-38 fighter planes attacked the railroad, doing significant damage to the boxcars. That night Harold felt restless.

Americans of the 90th Infantry Division taken as POW's in Germany, July 1944

His shoulder was sore, and the wooden bed was uncomfortable. The thought of having become a prisoner weighed deeply on him. He pulled out the New Testament that Annie had given him before basic and turned to his favorite verse, John 3:16. He prayed, "Lord, just get me home and let me be with Mom. I know she is praying for me. Amen." At daybreak German guards rushed into the building blowing whistles and yelling in German at the POWs. With great cruelty, they ordered the POWs to march to the train tracks and get into the boxcars, the very trains that had just been bombed by the Allies. The U.S. Army Air Forces VIII Bomber Command (later the U.S. Eighth Air Force) had been sent to destroy trains, train depots, and supply convoys heading towards the Cotentin Peninsula. American forces were approaching Saint-Lô, France, with elements of the 90th Division and the 357th Infantry leading the assault. PFC Frank and the two hundred captured POWs quietly loaded into the boxcars to avoid being shot by the guards.

The only ventilation was a five-inch hole in either end of the boxcar with barbed wire nailed on the outside of the hole. Many feared they wouldn't live after entering. One soldier on either side looked through the holes and warned when the fighters appeared. The heat of a tightly packed boxcar worked on the men. Harold heard many praying, others cursing, but an unusual calm came over him. Despite the continual throbbing from his shoulder, he managed a smile, convinced that at this moment his mom was praying. He was not the type of man to go insane. He looked at the others and thought to himself. "Somehow, someway I'm going to get home. I'm not going to let this get to me."

Around 1:00 p.m. the sound of airplanes brought shouts of alarm. The spotters in the boxcars yelled, "Quiet!" Suddenly the sound grew, and the spotter yelled, "P-38! There are several of them!" And a few seconds later he yelled, "He's coming this way! Damn it! Everyone take cover!"

All the POWs hit the floor. Harold balled up, covering his head. The .50-caliber rounds ripped through the boxcars, tearing the men apart. One POW was ripped open, exposing his spleen. Others were dismembered, some killed instantly. A few lingered, mortally wounded, groaning in pain. As quickly as the attack had started, it ended. Harold looked up. Apparently one of the spotters was hit. Another soldier took his spot and looked through the hole yelling out, "They're gone!"

Harold looked at his uniform now spotted with blood and other human remains. German guards opened the doors at gunpoint, ordering the POWs back into the buildings while the guards removed the bodies. PFC Frank counted sixteen soldiers that never left the car. As the guards entered the boxcar, Harold heard a few shots. Undoubtedly the wounded were being executed. Frank watched as a German Army sergeant walked up to the body of a U.S. Army paratrooper. He knelt down and examined his jump boots. Then he untied them and pulled them off. Putting them on his feet, he laughed and walked around talking in German to the other guards who seemed to agree with the sergeant's actions.

This became the daily routine for nearly two weeks. Some days no attacks occurred, and the men thankfully went back to their bunks. In all Harold witnessed and survived five attacks, each lasting ten to fifteen minutes. The last attack occurred without warning and caught everyone by surprise. Late on the afternoon of July 21, the guards were moving the POWs out of the box cars when out of nowhere a P-47 flew in and surprised everyone. Frank hit the ground yet again. He watched as .50-caliber rounds raked the area, cutting the right leg off the German guard wearing the U.S. Army jump boots. The rounds had cut the leg off just above boot height. Frank turned to another POW and said, "That was poetic justice."

CHAPTER 14

Train to Stalag IV B

N ear the end of July, they were packed into the boxcars again. This time it was different. The guards also boarded the train. Harold noticed a guard giving orders to the conductor. PFC Frank looked at the POWs and said, "I don't know where we're going but we're going somewhere." The train lurched forward, and the POWs were transported toward the German stalags. They were packed fifty in each car with a five-gallon bucket for a toilet. There was no provision for water. The heat and discomfort were aggravated by severe thirst. Motion sickness combined with the heat, and men continually vomited and worse. Soldiers made room for soldiers repeatedly, using the bucket to relieve diarrhea. Others were sickened by the smell and motion sickness. When the train stopped, a further insult was added. A German soldier dumped the contents from the bucket and, without rinsing it, filled it back up with water for the fifty to drink. This caused anger among the

POWs, whose words were silenced by the guards slamming the door closed and clasping the lock.

On July 29, the American POWs were marched through Paris escorted by eight German Army soldiers, four on each side. It looked like a parade, with heavily-armed German soldiers in the crowds to keep order. As PFC Frank's group of forty POWs arrived and looked at the crowd, they were stunned. Many in the crowd yelled insults and spit at them, and some threw rocks. PFC Frank's group of forty POWs were marched out of Paris and finally ordered into a barn where they slept on a dirt-and-straw floor. The next day they marched again to another train station and were placed in boxcars once again.

The heat of August and the horror of drinking from a five-gallon bucket formerly used as a latrine worked on the mental state of many of the POWs. The train finally stopped near Limburg, Germany at the POW camp Stalag XII A. PFC Frank's group was placed under guard in the open for a day and night. They loaded back up on a train and were taken to Stalag IV B near Dresden, Germany. After arriving at Stalag IV B, the POWs were checked in, and a German soldier painted a small, red triangle on the left leg and a large triangle on the back of each American soldier's olive-drab fatigues.

In Stalag IV B they had dirty water, little food, and lots of lice. There was no chain of command except German soldiers. PFC Frank passed the time observing the misery of POW life. When he could, he read the small Bible his mother had given him before basic training. The POWs were afraid to drink the water

Left: PFC Frank's Bible with Jones's and Stover's inscriptions written while POWs in Dresden
Right: PFC Frank's Bible—POW names that Frank wrote down while in captivity

for fear of contamination. The food was no more than turnips and potatoes prepared in various ways, but mostly boiled into a crude soup. Since Frank arrived in France, he had been warned not to drink the water without iodine pills, one per canteen. Here there was no choice.

Frank made a friend in PFC John Jones from Appleton City, Missouri. Each day for two weeks, the two watched other soldiers die, the bodies removed one by one. The bunks had little or no straw and were covered in lice, making sleep nearly impossible. There were many cases of German guards who had previously fought at the front severely torturing the POWs with a bayonet. Their captors also often used force to make the prisoners learn German.

Each day began with German guards blowing whistles. Failure to get up and move into formation resulted in beatings, partial bayonetting, and verbal abuse. PFC Frank still had some cigarettes and traded three to a Russian POW for his pocket-knife. Many of the POWs suffering from the abuse and scant food simply gave up. In the barracks at night, Frank heard many POWs mumbling, "We're all going to die." Frank looked at Jones one evening and said, "We need to get out of this place and try for something else."

The following morning, around August 15, German guards asked for volunteers for a work detail. Frank and Jones looked at each other and in desperation raised their hands. They were taken along with a few others back to the train yard and sent to Grossenheim (Dresden-Klotzsche), Germany, sixteen kilometers east of Dresden to a POW camp adjacent to a German fighter base and airfield.

At the Klotzsche Airfield work camp, PFC Frank and PFC Jones teamed up with two other POWS. One of these men was H.G. Barbazon from Atlanta, Georgia, and the other was Clyde Stover of Clarkrange, Tennessee. All four from the Southeast had volunteered to leave Stalag IV B prison camp for the work camp. They worked in a paper mill adjacent to Klotzsche Airfield and situated about 10 kilometers from Dresden. PFC Frank cut pulpwood into very small pieces, which was very similar to his old daily chore of keeping up the wood for Annie's wood cookstove. The main guard was a sixty-seven-year-old sergeant who was a World War I veteran and at least treated the men with some dignity. He had a corporal, however, who mistreated the POWs when the sergeant was away. In return for their labor, they would receive meat in the form of a horse head and neck once a month to feed the 107 working prisoners. The food was otherwise the same as that at Stalag IV B, a daily soup of turnips and potatoes.

Two POWs were selected to be the cooks. They had a small kitchen in the same building. The cooks were given one large twenty-five-gallon steam cooker. The day the horsehead was brought to the kitchen, the sixty-seven-year-old German sergeant added turnips, potatoes, and cabbage to go with it. The German sergeant told the cooks to make a stew. Every part was consumed, except for the eyes, windpipe, and bones. The POWs were given a handwashing pan for a plate. The two cooks dished the food out with a ladle. About a quart of stew was given to each POW. Due to the hunger concerns, the POWs told the cooks not to peel the potatoes. For the rest of the month the men ate only at dinner at noon and for supper at 7:00 p.m. No salt, pepper, or any other ingredients were available. The men never had a breakfast. The German guards threatened immediate death if any of the men were caught stealing food. PFC Frank noticed after two weeks that his weight was dropping quickly. After two months his clothing sagged everywhere, and his belt, fully notched, barely held up his pants. Its end hung out an extra eight to ten inches.

PFC Frank met a soldier from the 82nd who was from Arizona. He was a full-blooded Native American they called "Chief." Chief had been captured shortly before Frank. He looked at Frank and said, "I saw a German soldier shoot an airborne soldier all to pieces while hanging helpless in a tree.

Afterwards, I slit the throats of five German soldiers and left them in a line for other Germans to see."

The bunks were better than at IV B because the wooden bunks had straw-ticked bedding that was tucked into a linen bed. It opened in the center so you could replace or repair the straw. Outside the barracks was a short field surrounded by barbed-wire fences with concertina wire on top. There were two gates, one large and one small, just outside a guard shack manned by several guards, all well-armed. The first activity ordered by the guards was for PFC Frank and others to paint "POW" over the top of their building, and afterwards they were to begin work in the pulp mill.

About two weeks after arriving at the POW work camp, the Germans ordered the POWs to dig their own bomb shelter. Using pickaxes and shovels, the men dug a bunker outside the POW barracks about forty feet long and five feet wide and framed it with railroad crossties. The top crossties were placed tightly together with spikes driven through to join them. Then the men covered the bunker with four feet of dirt. This bunker held all 107 POWs.

Each day began at IV B with whistles at 6:00 a.m., and 107 men marched to the pulpwood factory a short distance away. The guards inspected and checked off each POW as he left and returned. Although there were more Army Air Force POWs than infantry, the German Army segregated them from regular Army POWs. The sixty-seven-year-old German sergeant was questioned once a month in an office for the German guards by a German Regular Army captain.

CHAPTER 15

Karl the German Supervisor

A civilian foreman by the name of Karl watched over PFC Frank and his three Southern buddies. After a few weeks, he came to trust Frank, who by this point had learned to speak rudimentary German.

In the middle of September, Karl came to PFC Frank and stated, "I will tell you some things about the war, but you can't tell any others or both of us will be killed." Harold agreed, and Karl said, "If you see another German coming through here, especially one in dress uniform or dressed up in any way, walk off, and don't talk with me. They're probably Gestapo, and if they find out I'm giving information, we will both be executed. Do you understand?"

"Yes, sir. Don't worry about me," replied Harold.

Karl looked at him and stated in a low voice, "Germany is losing the war. I don't know how soon, but U.S. and Russian troops are breaking through."

From then on Karl often talked with PFC Frank and, although risking danger, told Frank real news about the war.

Frank's shoulder wound had almost healed. This allowed Frank to work hard, which in turn impressed the foreman, who enjoyed talking with PFC Frank. As he told Frank the news, he made him swear to keep it to himself. Nevertheless, Frank quietly shared the news with the three friends that he trusted.

October 13, 1944 (Friday the thirteenth), was unusual. As with many times before, Frank awakened thinking he heard Annie's voice. Normally that indicated danger ahead, and he shook his head thinking, "It's Friday the thirteenth."

Just then, guards came into the barracks and called out, "PFC Frank!" Harold got up and was escorted by guards to the train station. The sixty-seven-year-old sergeant walked up and said, "You are going to a small hospital to have the bullet removed." On the train Frank noticed many deer in the vacant fields. He considered escaping. He realized that when Hitler ordered all guns seized years before this had caused exploding deer populations. Late that morning Frank arrived at a small hospital, which was really more of clinic than a hospital. The surgeon entered to remove the bullet from his shoulder. Beside him was a U.S. Army POW soldier who had had his leg amputated. The surgeon told Harold to lay stomach down on the table and told the guards to hold him down. Without using anesthesia, the German doctor cut into the wound as the two soldiers held Frank. The pain didn't bother PFC Frank until the doctor went into the incision with plyers to remove the bullet. It was lodged just under the shoulder blade. PFC Frank hollered as the bullet was removed and dropped into a pan.

After getting his voice back, Frank gasped to the doctor in German, "Captain, what are you going to do with that bullet?"

"I'll give it to you if you want it," the man replied.

"I want it!" PFC Frank exclaimed. "It's been in me for three months and I want to keep it!"

During the night the other soldier lay in anguished pain, seemingly from a phantom limb. The doctor would constantly enter the room to tell him he did not have the leg causing the pain. While in the hospital, PFC Frank managed to find extra food. For the first time, he received a Red Cross package that included seven packs of cigarettes, candy bars, and socks. This surprised Harold because the only POWs he had seen receive Red Cross packages were the few French POWs. Harold recovered from his surgery and two days later was sent back to the barracks. Though his arm was sore, he could now lift it over his head without any issues.

After returning from the hospital, Harold figured that Karl must have persuaded the sixty-seven-year-old sergeant to send him to have the bullet taken out of his shoulder because of how hard Frank worked even with it in there. One of the advantages of working in the pulpwood factory was that it had a shower and bathroom. The latrine had three commodes and four urinals, and the shower could hold up to a squad at a time. The Germans allowed the POWs one shower with soap every two weeks. The guards switched the groups every fifteen minutes.

They worked twelve-hour days, seven days a week except for Christmas. The weather elements meant nothing, so they worked in rain or snow. Although the accommodations were slightly better than IV B and the food occasionally better, they were always hungry, and Frank continuously lost weight.

On November 5, 1944, PFC Frank, who by now was healed from the wound and able to work, asked Karl, "Many Germans are good, hard-working people. How did the German people allow Hitler into power?"

"Hitler did it through intimidation and bypassing the Reichstag [German Congress]," Karl replied. Then he told Frank that "Unarmed German SS came and had us register all firearms. They said they didn't want the weapons but just wanted to make sure who had them. Then several months afterwards, a German Army halftrack came, and armed SS soldiers ordered me to give up the guns listed."

"I don't have the guns anymore," Karl had said.

But the SS officer had told Karl, "You have ten minutes to hand over the guns, or we will kill your wife and kids."

"They got the guns," Karl stated, while adding, "then we could do nothing."

Harold Frank never forgot the lessons from Karl.

Back in October, after PFC Frank returned from getting the bullet removed, the old German sergeant had given a guitar to a U.S. soldier from Tennessee who was a member of a four-brother bluegrass band called the Delmore Brothers. He played "The Tennessee Waltz," which became Harold's favorite song, comforting him the rest of his life. The Tennessean played so well that the guards would stay and listen. That night Harold Frank pulled out his New Testament. He had taken his shaving kit after his capture and pulled everything out of it to use as a cover for the Bible and letters. It protected them through the war.

The POWs normally stayed off the subject of food because a number of them constantly mumbled, "We're going to starve to death." Frank knew if you kept it on your mind that you might succumb to starvation from worry itself. He watched many times as the bodies of those who died from the effects of starvation were removed each day. But Frank said, "Each time I heard such comments, I would think: I'm too tough to starve or die. I'm going home because Mom has it even worse."

CHAPTER 16

Slingshot

G rowing up Harold Frank had learned at a young age how to make and perfect the slingshot he had used on many small birds and rabbits. The game he killed would be eaten around the fireplace at night. PFC Frank watched as Germans occasionally hunted rabbits with their Doberman Pinchers. Hitler had taken their guns, leaving this method as the only option. PFC Frank found a piece of a rubber inner tube in a scrap pile and immediately decided making a slingshot was a priority. While returning from a work detail, Frank found the perfect small bush, which resembled a sassafras tree, and took a perfect limb. Frank had traded three cigarettes to a Russian POW for the Russian's pocketknife earlier in Stalag IV B. He used this to complete the slingshot. He cut a piece of leather from the tongue of his boot to use as a patch. Other POWs from the northeast laughed and asked if he was going to kill the guards. "Of course not," he replied. Working as a team, the small group of Southerners watched for the brown German hares, which were often quite large. Harold pointed this out to PFC Jones of Missouri, also a country boy. When the guards weren't present, Frank would locate the den in the pile, kill the hare, and Jones or another would put it down a pants leg and return to the barracks to split dinner. Although this wasn't a great deal of food, it was enough to keep them alive.

When the pulpwood came from the railroad, it was six inches in diameter and two meters long. Frank would unload and place the wood in racks of twelve to fourteen logs. Then Harold ran an electric chain saw and cut the logs in half. He stacked them in straight piles fifty-to-one-hundred-feet long, six-to-eight-feet high. The German pilots had a containment area for the rabbits they used exclusively for fur liners inside the pilot's flight jackets. The POWs were under strict orders to never approach this rabbit containment area. Opening the door would result in the death of the POW. Still, Frank would find ways to conceal himself around stacks of pallets or wood and take the left-over turnips or carrots that were fed to the rabbits. "Somehow a country boy will find a way to survive." What was more, the slingshot proved invaluable and remain undetected.

PFC Frank was allowed to write four letters home as a POW, and each was limited to nothing more than a card. The letters were heavily censored, so the POW was told to keep the language as ordinary as possible, or it might not be sent at all.

Back in North Carolina, the Frank family was at first told that PFC Harold Frank was missing in action. Four months later his status was changed to POW. The War Department notification of the change in status caused excitement for the Franks, but led to worry too. Edward had heard reports of poor conditions in German camps. Annie was instructed that in order for a letter to reach Harold she would have to keep her language as bland as possible to avoid German censorship of incoming mail.

The first letter from Annie was dated November 22, 1944. Annie explained that word of Harold being a POW had just arrived that day. Annie wrote: "Keep your chin up and don't give up. For we are all thinking about you." Annie cautiously warned Harold that her writing might be bland by stating, "But you know we have to go by rules now. Will write more soon. As ever with lots of Love, From Mom." Harold was relieved and excited to have a piece of home with him, and each day he would pull the letter back out and read it. He also shared the words from home with PFC Barbazon, PFC Jones, and PFC Stover. Each night PFC Frank opened his Bible and turned to his favorite scripture, John 3:16. To protect the letter and Bible, Frank, having removed the contents of his shaving kit, carefully folded the letter and secured it inside, protected from weather and work.

One day as the POWs came into the paper mill, some of the German secretaries in the factory caused a scene. They strutted around sticking out their chests and flirting with the POWs. PFC Frank knew immediate discipline would occur if they communicated back in any way. The women also knew this as they

WRITE VERY CLEARLY WITHIN THE LINES. IN ORDER TO EXPEDITE
CENSORSHIP, LETTERS SHOULD BE TYPED OR PRINTED IN BLOCK CAPITALS.

Nov. 2 2, 1944

Dear Harold,

Hope you are well
and in good health, we are all
well at home sure would
like to see you. I received the
first card you wrote after you
was captured to day. sure was
glad to hear from you and
hope you can soon come home.
keep your chin up and dont
give up. for we are all thinking
about you, and doing ever thing
we can to send you a ~~package~~
package, but you know we
have to go by rules now. will
write more soon. as ever with
lots of love from MOM.

Letter from Annie to POW Harold Frank, November 22, 1944

tried to entice the men. PFC Frank looked at PFC Jones and said, "They want to see us get beaten by the guards." The secretaries and female mill workers thought this quite amusing. But this was not all. While the men worked, the local Hitler Youth would taunt the POWs and throw rocks at them while they stacked wood. The German guards stood and laughed as the POWs attempted to dodge the stoning.

A few days later, Harold Frank received another letter from home, this one dated November 26, 1944. Harold smiled, knowing it was the Sunday just after Thanksgiving. Harold paused as he read. From the contents, he realized that one of his cards must have made it home. But he also learned that his good friend Artis Cecil had been wounded. Annie wrote, "Well son you asked about Artis Cecil a good while ago. He has been wounded and is back over here now in a hospital and is at home for a few days." A few lines later, Annie told Harold that Edward had informed Artis of Harold's POW status. Then Annie ended with, "Am still praying for you to soon get home. So bye for now, with lots of love from Mom," which she underlined.

PFC Frank knew Annie was praying for him. He felt that the timely arrival of the U.S. Army medic who helped him heal his wound was a direct result of divine intervention. Annie felt it was her job to try to comfort but at the same time lift Harold's spirit without specifically mentioning the war. In her own way, she notified Harold that America was doing well. In a letter dated November 30, 1944, Annie mentioned: "We diden get to kill our hogs the other day when I told you we might. It rained

WRITE VERY CLEARLY WITHIN THE LINES. IN ORDER TO EXPEDITE
CENSORSHIP, LETTERS SHOULD BE TYPED OR PRINTED IN BLOCK CAPITALS.

Nov 30, 1944

Dearest Harold,
                    hope you are
well and in Good Health.
we are all well here
at home.
we diden Get to Kill our hogs
the other day when I told
you we Might it rained so
Much, Guess we will Kill
tomorrow as it is very
cold here tonight. archie
said tell you He went to
deer hunting diden Get
no deer but saved his
Shirt tail diden Get his
Shirt cut off Like dad
did last year.

Jean said tell you that She
is working hard in her
school books and is
Getting along alright at
School She has A Good
teacher this year dad has
Just come in from Tyro and
said Rab wanted to know
how you was Getting along
ever body around is anxious to
hear from you but we cant
tell them much as we have
CONTINUE ON TOP PANEL OVERLEAF

Letter from Annie to POW Harold Frank, November 30, 1944

so much. Guess we will kill tomorrow as it is very cold here tonight." Then she included that Harold's little brother had gone hunting. "Archie said to tell you he went too deer hunting's diden get no deer but saved his shirt tail and diden get his shirt cut off like dad did last year." Harold laughed and paused, looking at the bed he had covered with the very little straw available. He heard other POWs mumbling, "We're going to starve to death. I'm hungry." Harold looked back at the letter and slowly read the last line where Annie stated: "We all would like so much to see you. So by for this time. Love as ever from Mom." PFC Frank looked over at PFC Barbazon and said, "I ain't gonna die here. I'm too damn tough. Somehow we're going to get home."

Annie wrote in a letter dated December 5, 1944, that: "I received your card yesterday that you wrote me Sept 8th and sure was glad to hear from you." Then Harold shook his head as he read: "Glad you are getting plenty to eat." Harold knew after his capture that Annie would be worried to death if she only knew what had happened to him. He purposely refused to mention his wounding, harsh conditions, work requirements, and especially starvation. Annie skipped a line as if to recognize she knew better and asked if Harold was "getting my letter as I have been sending you one most every day since Nov 1." Annie ended that same letter with "keep your chin up and you will be okay. For I am praying for you continually."

In late December many of the guards appeared more humorous, but also taunted the POWs continually. The German children still threw rocks at the POWs as they worked in the

WRITE VERY CLEARLY WITHIN THE LINES. IN ORDER TO EXPEDITE
CENSORSHIP, LETTERS SHOULD BE TYPED OR PRINTED IN BLOCK CAPITALS.

Dec. 16 1944

Dear Harold.
                hope you are
Well and feeling fine.
We are all Well here at
home. and dad has gone
to work has to work ever
Sat any more. Well
Archie thinks he is in
Pig Heaven now as he has
bought him a ? but not
a New one. I dont guess
naomi will come home for
the week as the Buses
are so crowded. we are
still haveing some very cold
weather I do hope the
weather where you are is
not so cold.
Well son as xmas is just
a week off and you away
I dont know what we
will do for xmas but
guess it will just be anoth[er]
day with me this will be
two xmases with out you
and it wont seem right
Till we can all be together
again. we are all thinking
about you. dont forget
That my Prayers are for

CONTINUE ON TOP PANEL OVERLEAF

Letter from Annie to POW Harold Frank, December 16, 1944—The day
the Battle of Bulge began and Christmas 1944

pulpwood yard. The POWs knew something was up. PFC Frank was given another letter that revealed that very few letters or cards he gave to the guards were making it home. PFC Frank received a letter from Annie dated December 16, 1944. Harold looked somewhat depressed as he read: "Son as xmas is just a week off and you away I don't know what we will do for xmas but guess it will just be another day with me this will be two xmases with out you and it want seem right till we can all be together again. We are all thinking about you don't forget that my prayers are for you and with you all the time." Annie ended with a plea that: "I do hope you are getting my letters. So by for now with lots of love from Mom." The next morning Harold found out why the taunting was occurring.

PFC Frank and the other POWs now numbered 105 after two had died from a combination of disease, starvation, and exhaustion. Frank overheard German soldiers bragging about fighting in the Ardennes.

As the POWs marched by the guard station and gate to the pulp yard, several guards yelled, "You will never see home again because the German Army is kicking American ass."

PFC Frank, reflecting on the letter from Annie, replied back, "That's what you think! Just wait till General Patton gets here. Then we'll see whose ass is being kicked!"

In reality the struggle the German soldiers referred to became known as the Battle of the Bulge.

After the encounter with the guard, Karl, the German foreman, told PFC Frank, "It doesn't matter. Germany doesn't have the fuel to keep our tanks running, so it's just a matter of time."

The following day was Sunday, December 24, and Christmas Eve. After returning from the pulp factory, the guards said they would be off Christmas Day. That night Harold removed his Bible from the shaving kit and turned to Luke chapter two and read the Christmas story. Afterwards PFC Frank, PFC Jones, PFC Barbazon, and PFC Stover rested together and talked about what each ate for Christmas back home. Turkey was not the common Thanksgiving meal everywhere. Clyde and Barbazon talked about barbecuing whole hog, while Frank and Jones reminisced about his mother's chicken roasting.

Frank smiled at the three other men and said, "My Pap would like some mud turtle, and Uncle Pharris would climb the wall for opossum!"

The four laughed, but some from the northeast who had overheard hollered, "You Rebs aren't right!"

"You'd eat it now and don't deny it!" Frank replied.

The talk became quiet as the bluegrass picker took the guitar and played "Silent Night." Afterwards, as had become custom, the last song was "The Tennessee Waltz."

On Tuesday, December 26, 1944, the POWs noticed the guards were not as jolly and seemed quiet as they headed to the pulp yard. When Frank entered the pulp factory, Karl called over to him, "Come over here, please." When PFC Frank walked up, Karl said, "The German Army in the Ardennes has been driven back by the American Army."

"Sounds like General Patton," Frank observed.

Karl noticed that Harold had a watch and asked, "Did you have that watch back in America?"

"Yes, but it's been broke ever since I got captured." He handed the watch to Karl and said, "It's a seven-jewel Waltham. My dad gave it to me as the oldest boy."

Karl looked it over and said, "I'll have it fixed, but it may take me a few days."

"I trust you and would be grateful if it worked again," Frank said.

Three days later, while PFC Frank was working in the pulp mill yard, Karl approached him and said, "I've got your watch fixed," and then handed it back to Frank.

"Karl, this means a lot to me, and I really appreciate this," Harold said, and then he went back to work cutting pulpwood.

CHAPTER 17

Bombing of Dresden

A ir attacks had picked up in the area during November 1944, which did create some concern with the Me 109 airfield less than a thousand yards away. PFC Frank watched time and again as B-17 bombers flew overhead, some blown half in two from the flak of antiaircraft guns or from the Me 109 fighters. Many times no one bailed out, and, on several occasions, the few that parachuted were shot by the German Me 109 fighters. These bombers were not bombing Dresden but heading to other targets.

In mid-January PFC Frank received what would be the last letter from home. Annie wrote on January 10, 1944, that she had received two cards from Harold that were dated October. The news brightened PFC Frank's outlook, and he smiled when Annie wrote that: "Joe is still taking care of your dog for you so you and him can go hunting someday." Towards the end of the

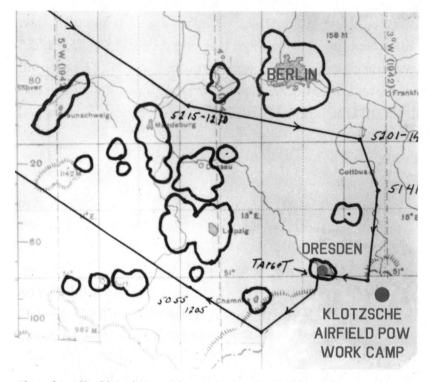

Chart for Allied bombing raid on Dresden, overlaid with locations of the
Klotzsche Airfield POW work camp and nearby cities

letter Harold paused and read on: "We all hope you will soon
be back with us again."

By February of 1945, many of the German antiaircraft
guns had been removed from areas near Dresden and placed
on railcars for use along the Russian front. PFC Frank, as well
as the other POWs, noticed the stockpile of military equipment,
especially artillery, in the railyard. By the agreement at the
Casablanca Conference, the British Air Force would bomb by

night, and the U.S. Army Air Forces would bomb by day. Harold was awaked to the sound of Annie's voice, "Harold." He glanced over at PFC Jones and PFC Stover. The air-raid sirens went off, and the guards were not immediately present, so Frank and Jones ran out and climbed on top of scrapped paper bales that were about thirty feet high to try to get a glimpse of what was happening before going into the bunker. It was February 13, 1945, at 0200.

Air-raid sirens continued to blare as the POWs scrambled to their bombing shelter. In the excitement of scrambling for cover and listening to the approaching noise of bombers, the German guards had failed to order the POWs into their separate shelter. All thought the airfield was being hit. Frank and Jones ran on top of a paper bale and yelled, "It's British Lancaster Bombers!"

PFC Jones looked at PFC Frank and said, "Looks like they're going to hit the airfield. It sounds like a lot of bombers."

About that time a flair was dropped from somewhere in the sky, and the bombers began to turn. PFC Frank looked at Jones and said "Oh, Lordy, they're heading straight into Dresden."

The British dropped flairs, and the British four-engine Lancaster Bombers turned at the flairs and made the final sixteen kilometers. A continuous roar of bombers followed. Within a few minutes, explosions, flashes of fire, and the constant shaking of ground reached them. It sounded like very large, severe thunderstorms approaching from the southwest, or a mild earthquake. The deafening roar of the bombers and subsequent release of the bombs lasted three and a half hours, until about

0530. At daylight, Frank and Jones climbed off the bales to avoid being seen by the guards and slipped into the shelter, where they told the POWs, "They are bombing the hell out of that town over there."

All cheered at the bombing finally coming this far into Germany. Frank looked at Stover and Barbazon and stated, "If they're bombing this far into Germany, the war must be coming to an end."

The thought of a final end raised excitement among the POWs and they chanted, "The U.S. Army will be here soon!"

"It's going to be Patton!" Harold yelled.

At 0600 the POWs were ordered back to work. They came out and looked at the smoke pluming in the distance as they headed to the pulp mill.

The air-raid sirens sounded once again, and the POWs heard the roar, then saw the sight of hundreds of U.S. Army Air Forces B-17s flying in formation. They were not ordered into bunkers again. It was apparent that the city, not the airfield, was the target. PFC Jones and PFC Frank rejoiced quietly until noon. At that time both of them witnessed the downing of two B-17s. One was blown in half, and the other bomber's tail section blew apart. No men parachuted as the planes went down. Near dark on February 13, the bombing stopped. The smoke cleared, but as night fell it was replaced by a large glow from the direction of the burning city of Dresden.

A young German Army corporal who was a guard at the camp had returned on the seventeenth from the bombing, looking angry and upset. He shouted obscenities at all the POWs. Several guards approached the young corporal and calmed him down for fear he was going to open fire on the prisoners. Karl later told PFC Frank that the sergeant of the guard had transferred the man quickly, fearing that he would kill the POWs. The German soldier's family and home had disappeared during the bombing.

At the beginning of March, Frank and Jones were working in the paper mill yard unloading wood when a loud sound startled everyone. A ME 262 fighter flew low over the airfield and then suddenly straight up into the sky with a roar and disappeared. Frank and Jones were stunned and stared at each other.

At the same time they said, "What the hell was that?"

Noticeably surprised, Harold said, "The Germans have some kind of new plane!"

Jones said, "It didn't have any props but looked like two engines on the wings."

"Yeah, and it was moving faster than anything I've ever seen," replied Frank.

"Well, Frank, let's hope it's the only one the Nazis have."

The two returned to stacking pulpwood.

CHAPTER 18

The March of Death:
Evacuation and Escape Attempt

At the end of March, PFC Frank and the others knew the war was getting close. There were constant artillery sounds in the far distance. The Russian front was closing in each day. The destruction of Dresden left roads around the area full of homeless refugees fleeing from Russian forces after the bombing. Inside the POW camp, work continued. The paper mill still functioned, and the airfields got busier as German fighters flew toward the Russian advance.

Thursday, April 17, at daybreak there wasn't time for air-raid sirens as suddenly there was a low-level attack on Klotzsche by sixteen U.S. Army Air Forces P-51s and P-47s from the VIII Fighter Command. P-51s attacked the airfield adjacent to the POW building and went after the German aircraft caught on the ground. PFC Frank, PFC Barbazon, and PFC Clark were outside unloading pulpwood from the railroad flatcars. Four

U.S. P-47 fighters attacked, strafing the runway and planes parked on the airfield. Then there was an explosion in the air, and Frank watched one of the P-47s smoking. It crashed out of sight. After a few minutes, the fighters disappeared and PFC Frank, PFC Jones, PFC Stover, and PFC Barbazon counted at least thirty-one German planes either destroyed or on fire, including Fw 190s, Me 410s, Ju 88s, and seven others they could no longer recognize.

The men went back to work, but by 11:00 a.m. eight more U.S. fighters appeared, once again a mix of P-47s and P-51s. They attacked as the air-raid siren on the airfield went off. More German planes were destroyed along with the loss of yet another U.S. fighter that was hit and went down out of sight. Remarkably, a few German planes and some of the barracks were still intact. Meanwhile, the three U.S. soldiers were ordered back to work in the pulp yard.

Around 1530, as many as sixteen U.S. fighters appeared again. Several German planes tried to get off the ground but were destroyed in the attempt. In minutes all the German aircraft were destroyed. The U.S. fighters concentrated on the barracks. The POW barrack was the last building, about eight hundred yards from the runway. Frank told Jones and Barbazon, "We ain't going to be here much longer. If the fighters are coming in this close now, the war must be coming to an end." As the evening approached, not a German plane was left untouched. All the barracks were on fire except the one marked POW. The POWs were locked up in the barracks. PFC Frank never saw Karl again.

PFC Harold Frank's Reichsmark bill he carried as POW

On Friday afternoon Russian artillery was heard again but much louder than previous days. The roads near the POW Camp were filled with more refugees. On Saturday, April 19, the POWs were forced to evacuate from the work camp. They marched around a Dresden that was impassable and in complete ruins. With very little food or rest, they were pushed into Czechoslovakia. Many times PFC Frank remembered falling asleep while walking, only to be awakened by a horse behind him that would gently nudge him on the back, waking him up as he continued to stumble onward.

As a common practice the POWs couldn't break ranks. They were forced to use the road as a bathroom or be killed. They began the march with 105 of the POWs. PFC Frank, PFC Jones, PFC Stover, and PFC Barbazon were near the front of the column. German police dogs barked, and there was an occasional shot from a German rifle. PFC Frank and his three buddies concentrated on encouraging one another to keep moving.

They marched nonstop from Saturday to Tuesday. PFC Frank and his small group of buddies were soon exhausted, but kept encouraging each other with words like, "Hang on," "Don't give up," and, "You can make it." In many cases Frank was sleep-walking, and again the horse would wake him from behind with a nudge in his back. Getting through the march alive was an achievement in itself. Late on Sunday, the artillery booms grew louder. Neither the Germans nor the POWs wanted to be captured by Russian troops.

During the day Frank saw other German soldiers leading prisoners away. The column of prisoners didn't appear to be former soldiers, and German could be heard in their ranks. Frank called out to the sixty-seven-year-old sergeant and asked who they were. The sergeant looked for a second and replied calmly, "They are political prisoners." Frank was stunned. Even though they were German citizens, they were half naked and near death. As the unceasing walk continued, they passed one horse team after another pulling refugees. The desperate effort to move away from the Russians caused many of the horses to collapse and die from exhaustion. Then the families would climb off and continue the walk. The memory of the terror Harold witnessed and the despair in every eye became permanently seared in his mind. The POWs that couldn't make the march, the police dogs barking, and the German rifle fire would fill his dreams for decades. The column marched for many miles. They crossed into Czechoslovakia and then turned back into Germany and finally stopped on Tuesday, April 22, at about 0700. The POWs were ordered to rest. They immediately collapsed and drank a bit of water. The German guards went into a group of the resting POWs. Harold noticed a U.S. Army helmet and liner that had apparently rolled down the hill into a ditch nearby. He quickly got the two pieces and put it on his head.

"We've got to be getting close to the lines." PFC Frank thought that now he could use the helmet to get food or water. Frank was now more fluent in German and overheard the conversation taking place between the guards. He heard the guards say they had arranged sites that were mostly barns. They discussed the move away from Dresden toward Czechoslovakia. Then in loose translation Harold overheard the guards mentioning Frankfurt. Harold remembered this as the worst experience of the POW period. He turned to Jones and said, "Better rest. According to what I picked up on, they're moving us to prearranged areas somewhere near Czechoslovakia or Frankfurt." Jones just nodded as the two laid down and propped up their feet to get pressure off the pads.

On April 23, during the march to the next resting point, PFC Barbazon collapsed. His two companions noticed an abandoned flat cart with wheels and broke ranks to place PFC Barbazon in it. They pulled him along, and the guards didn't seem to care. That night the temperatures plunged. In the barns, the three men had buttoned two coats together and laid one down to sleep on. Jones and Barbazon were on the coat. Frank covered them in hay then crawled between them. They were starving as they entered the barns, when Frank noticed a hen in nearby barnyard and motioned to Jones. Then Frank pulled out his slingshot. The guards didn't notice Frank's killing the hen. He told Jones to grab the dead hen before its blood spattered on the ground. Jones did so and concealed their catch. That night they cooked hen stew using the helmet for a pot. The sixty-seven-year-old sergeant came in and saw the stew.

Frank said, "We're eating potatoes."

The sergeant stuck a spoon in the stew and said, "Das ist eine Henne," but he let them eat.

On April 27, as the march continued, PFC Frank and PFC Jones saw an opportunity to escape. The group of POWs were told to enter a barn and go into the loft to sleep. They were all exhausted. After the men had entered the loft, the guards closed the barn door. Harold heard a latch being turned or locked. The guards remained outside. During the night, the temperature turned sharply colder as the four tried to sleep in the straw. PFC Frank and PFC Jones were unable to get to sleep. They decided to use this opportunity to get milk from some Holstein cows below, which Frank had identified by their black and white spots. Frank pulled off his helmet and whispered, "Let's get some milk while we can." The two slid down a chute from the loft beside the cows. Harold removed his helmet to catch the milk. He had the most milking experience and went to work. After filling the helmet half full, Frank drank half and gave the rest to Jones.

Fortified with milk, the two went back into the loft where they found a loose plank. The rest of the POWs were sound asleep. Working together, they managed to carefully and quietly pull the plank out and rolled through the plank opening. Harold went first, dangling down the side and falling to the ground. Then John Jones did the same. The two ventured a few miles as it neared daylight. They came upon a small farmhouse, and they heard talking inside. The two slipped around the house and into the darkness, walking until daylight, when they hid in some woods. After darkness fell again, they walked around a small village and carefully moved through the night across the farmland. The two were completely lost, and they went into a barn and rested in the loft on the hay for a short nap. The two woke up a few hours later. It was still dark. "We've got to get out of here before daylight," Frank said. From a small tree line they watched a German family planting seed potato. When the family had finished and walked back into the house, Frank and Jones dashed into the garden to dig up six or seven potatoes. They ate them raw.

They decided to cautiously continue to travel by day. Later that morning the two came within sight of railroad tracks and spotted workers walking to a small shop adjacent to the tracks.

They patiently watched a group of workers going in and out of a repair shop, but waited until all had ventured out from the shop. The workers then gathered on a pump car and disappeared down the tracks. Quickly, the two POWs ran into the shop and found where they had left their lunches. Grabbing the lunches, they darted back into the woods. The two continued several more miles while eating sandwiches and a few carrots.

They moved in what they thought was the direction of Frankfurt, although they had no map of any kind. Just being apprehended with a map would bring certain death. Up on a hill, Frank and Jones noticed approximately one hundred German soldiers digging foxholes. Several hundred yards away, they saw a small dirt road with two guards at an intersection in the village. The guards had the road blocked. Harold told Jones that, "We can't go around, or we'll run into the Germans digging in." Frank remembered a story handed down from family history. At the end of the Civil War, one of Harold's uncles was walking home after the Confederacy surrendered. Near home, Federal guards blocked the bridge crossing the Yadkin River and made the Confederate soldiers wade the river. Harold's uncle got a hold of some pokeberries that were purple in color. Dotting his face with them, he turned to another traveling with him and did the same to his face. They walked to the guards, who stood up to stop them. Loudly, the two yelled, "Smallpox!" and pointed at their faces. The guards scattered out of the way and told the two to pass on through. Somehow a country boy will find a way.

"I've got an idea, just follow me," said PFC Frank.

As they headed onto the road PFC Jones asked quietly, "What's the plan?"

"We're a work detail that's been called out yonder past the guards to help a farmer. If we don't get there, the farmer will turn us in. Let me do the talking because I speak better German."

As the two approached the guard, PFC Frank informed the German soldier that they were a work detail going beyond to a farm. If they didn't get there soon, they would be turned in. After some back and forth questioning, he convinced the guards to let them go. As the two POWs had walked about fifty feet, a German officer ran out to the men in anger. He stopped them and ordered them into the guard building. PFC Frank yelled at him in German with disgust and lots of profanity. He told the German officer about how much trouble they would be in if they didn't make it to the work detail.

The officer looked up and said in perfect English. "I know you two are escaped U.S. POWs. You might as well admit to it."

Frank looked at Jones and said, "He can speak better English than I can."

While shaking his head and placing his hand on Jones's shoulder, he said, "I tried, but he was smarter than the Yankees were."

The German officer asked which camp they were from, and Frank told him. The two were immediately escorted by foot for several miles to a barn where the two recognized that same sixty-seven-year-old German sergeant.

The sergeant laughed while looking at the two and stated, "The Englishmen and French leave and don't return, but the Americans come back."

"It wasn't our choice, or we would've been gone," Frank replied.

The other POWs just laughed. One responded, "You all are lucky to be back."

Off in the distance the sound of artillery could be heard once again. The German guards looked at each other and commented that it was the Russians getting closer. The POWs continued to walk along with the many refugees fleeing from Russian attacks. PFC Barbazon, the soldier from Atlanta, Georgia, collapsed again from exhaustion. PFC Frank and PFC Jones quickly found another farm wagon. The team put him in it, and Frank pulled the wagon. The group continued to walk.

Barbazon looked at Frank and Jones, telling them both, "I was hoping you two had made it to the front lines."

Harold just shook his head and said, "We came close, but couldn't make it."

They rested that night and the following morning, and on May 5, they heard artillery fire from other directions.

CHAPTER 19

General Eisenhower and Lucky Strikes

O n May 7, 1944, the men were ordered up by the guards to continue to march. During the morning, the guards appeared in civilian clothes and ordered the remaining seventy POWs to get up. The sixty-seven-year-old sergeant stated, "We've received word that the war is over. You POWs are free to leave." They looked at each other and walked cautiously at first, thinking they would be shot.

The sergeant yelled, "It's over! Go!"

PFC Frank turned to the sergeant and said, "You above all the others tried to treat us fair and take care of us. You should come with us. There's nothing left behind but the Russians."

The old sergeant said, "Frank, this is my home, and I will stay. It's time for you to go home to America and return to your family."

With that the POWs walked towards a small village and found a bakery. Together they pulled together a few German marks they'd managed to gather and bought bread. Walking out together, they proceeded down the road pulling the wagon carrying PFC Barbazon.

A U.S. Army jeep came up, and a sergeant from General Patton's Third Army jumped out when he recognized the POWs. He told them to stop and rest.

The sergeant looked at PFC Frank and asked, "What's your name and what unit are you with?"

"PFC Harold Frank, Company G, 2nd Battalion, 357th Infantry," he replied.

"Where are you from?" said the sergeant.

"Tyro, North Carolina."

"Hey, 'Fox Hole,' we have a Tar Heel."

Frank looked to see a soldier coming up to the Army jeep with full canteens.

The sergeant glanced at Frank and laughed, "You can trace every mile of General Patton's Third Army by his foxholes. That's why we call him, 'Fox Hole Kilby.'"

The soldier walked up to Frank, handed him a canteen and said, "Yeah, but I'm still alive!" Looking at Frank, he asked, "Where did you get captured?"

"Somewhere near Beacoudray, France. I was with the 357th Infantry leading a patrol with my BAR to find two companies that had got cut off. We got into a firefight. I was shot in the shoulder and ran out of ammo." Pausing and shaking his head while looking at Fox Hole Kilby he said, "And afterwards we were captured. The Krauts executed one of us. He was wounded in the leg and couldn't walk. The four of us here spent ten months as POWs near Dresden. We witnessed a hell of a bombing. The city became a heap of ashes, but somehow we survived it. Out of one hundred seven prisoners, only seventy survived."

He caught his breath and paused; then PFC Jones looked at the sergeant and said, "FUBAR."

The sergeant looked at the former POWs and said, "Good to have you boys back. Just sit down and rest. We've got trucks coming to pick you up. You boys are skin and bones, but I think we can pull together some Army fatigues and burn that POW shit because you're with Patton now."

"I'll find a bar of soap in the hotel that we're putting you boys in," replied Fox Hole Kilby.

Soon two U.S. Army trucks appeared and pulled over. The sergeant along with Fox Hole Kilby helped the POWs into the trucks.

Fox Hole asked Frank, "Where in North Carolina are you from?"

"Near Lexington in Davidson County," Frank replied.

Fox Hole laughed and said, "We're not far apart. I'm from Iredell County near Statesville."

The trucks left, and after a few miles the vehicles stopped. The men unloaded and walked into the hotel. When the sergeant walked in, he said, "You all find a room. They're all clean with fresh sheets, but only one shower works. It's on the bottom floor." The Army had converted the hotel into four-man rooms equipped with folding cots. The POWs spent their first night in real beds with sheets and blankets.

PFC Frank said, "I haven't slept in a real bed with white sheets in a year. I've slept in foxholes, dirt, and hay for too long."

Fox Hole came into PFC Frank's room and said, "Got you boys a set of fatigues, socks, boots, and soap!"

Frank chimed in, "Time to get leathered up! But we need something to eat!"

"No worries," Fox Hole said. "The cooks are taking care of y'all. Just get cleaned up and rest. Someone will be by to take y'all to the mess tent behind the hotel."

After they showered and got cleaned, another soldier came and took the boys to chow. Their first meal since liberation was baked beans with pieces of bacon and pork fat. The four ate all they could and returned to their room. Not long after returning and laying in the sheets, all four developed severe stomach cramps. Five medics came in and massaged their stomachs and warned each of the liberated soldiers not to eat large amounts for several weeks. After that Harold slept without waking until late in the morning.

About 10:00 a.m. gunfire erupted, causing panic. PFC Frank quickly got into the fatigues and ran out of the hotel. A U.S. Army sergeant was guarding a large pile of captured German weapons. During the morning, Germans wearing civilian clothes were attempting to steal some of those weapons. Only the sergeant was on guard then, and he was attempting to force the Germans away.

When the sergeant saw Frank and his buddies, he yelled, "Pick up some of these weapons and help me! If not, I'm going to have to shoot 'em!"

Frank grabbed a Mauser and yelled a few German words at them they would understand. This caused them to flee. Afterwards Frank and Jones counted the liberated POWs and realized that thirty-seven of the POWs had not survived the forced march.

About two weeks later they were transported to an airfield and loaded into a C-47. A soldier helped Frank and Jones carry Barbazon into the holding area. He looked at the three and stated, "This plane was one of the C-47s carrying airborne during the D-day invasion. Find a place and sit down. You all are heading to Camp Lucky Strike near Janville, France." The plane took off, and the flight was smooth until nearing Janville. There it had to circle several times before being cleared to land. The constant turning brought back the motion sickness reminiscent of D-Day. Finally, and just in time for the men to avoid vomiting, the C-47 landed.

Shortly after arriving, the men unloaded and were assigned to different tents. PFC Frank and the other former POWs were ordered to a supply tent and given new uniforms and boots. That evening while heading to the chow line, Frank and the soldiers with him were called to attention. General Eisenhower was present. He announced that he would eat with them first and would talk afterwards. Frank and the other POWs went into the line to receive food. He watched as the cook placed a small spoonful of butterscotch pudding on his tray.

In anger Frank looked at the cook and said, "Let me have some more of the pudding. I haven't had anything like this in nearly ten months."

"I'm in charge of the pudding," the cook replied. "You'll eat what I give you."

General Eisenhower heard what was transpiring between Frank and the cook. Immediately he walked up to the cook and said, "You give the man what he asked."

The cook at first said, "No!" Then he looked up and saw the five stars and quickly changed his tune. "Yes, sir, boss! Yes, sir, boss!"

Frank cheered, clapped his hands, and said, "Thank God for those five stars!"

While the men were eating, General Eisenhower stood up and looked at PFC Frank and the men around him. He told them, "Boys, I'm going to let all of you call home. But go ahead and eat first." After eating, the POWs were to be given time to call home.

The poor health condition of many of the POWs needed immediate attention, however. The scant diet they had endured resulted in their experiencing severe stomach pains, and several left and threw up after eating. One of the medics looked at Frank and said, "I know all of you are hungry, but for next few days only eat small amounts very slowly. Afterwards lay down and massage your stomachs."

It was hard to tell men who had been reduced to sharing one horsehead per month with 107 others, along with watered-down turnip or potato soup, that at the sight of real food they should only eat small samples. Once they had recovered from the stomach pains, the men headed to the phone line.

When Harold made his way to the phone at Camp Lucky Strikes, a thousand thoughts and feelings flooded his mind. So much had happened to him, and in such a short amount of time. Just a year ago, he'd left his parents at Fort Meade and prepared for the D-Day invasion. Shortly after that he went into intense combat for thirty straight days—combat that virtually wiped out most of his company, along with a large part of the 357th. A German sniper shot him in the shoulder. Wounded and captured, he was miraculously kept alive with the help of a captured American medic. Incredibly, he was lucky enough to survive ten months in a German POW workcamp, train attacks, bombings, starvation, an escape attempt, recapture, and a seemingly endless forced march, and now he was holding a phone in his hand about to call home. Frank picked up the phone and gave the number of his sister to the operator. In a few moments he heard Naomi's voice.

"Hello," she answered, then, with a pause, she said, "Hello," once more.

"Naomi, this is Harold. I can't talk long because there is a line of soldiers waiting. I'm all right! Tell Mom and Dad that I'm back in the U.S. Army, and I'll be home soon."

Naomi, tearful and excited, said, "Thank God, and I'll tell Mom and Dad."

Both said a quick goodbye and hung up.

He didn't want to tell them anything about his POW life or that he had been wounded. It would've particularly grieved his mom, Annie, too much. She had already endured a son going to war, then missing in action—possibly dead—and finally a POW.

While waiting for the ship ride back to the United States, many of the liberated POWs were given passes to go into town. The officers warned those who took the passes, "You men are going to be shipped out of the country and going home. Be careful if you take a pass." He paused and looking stern he told the men, "Don't catch anything. The war has just ended, and sanitation is shit. Living conditions are hell. Do not get any venereal diseases. Be careful, or you'll be stuck here even longer."

Most of the men heeded the warning. This included PFC Frank. After the officer left, one group stated they didn't care. Frank overheard one say, "I've been stuck in a POW camp, starved, and nearly dead. I'm going to town and find a woman."

Frank looked on as the men urged him to go. Then he said to them, "No, I'm going to rest and get ready to come home, but y'all have fun and hopefully find a nice French woman."

The men cheered and patted Frank's shoulder. Several yelled, "Hold the fort till we come back tomorrow."

The next morning all had made it back in good spirits before morning. One of the men looked at Frank while sitting on his bunk and said, "Frank, you said you were with the 357th Infantry at Utah Beach?"

"That's right. We came in behind the 4th Infantry."

"Well, did you remember French women being in the bunkers with the Krauts?"

PFC Frank looked and quickly responded, "Yeah, I had to shoot several. They grabbed rifles and shot at us!"

"When we went into town yesterday evening, I saw women whose heads were shaved, and the other women stayed away from them. The woman I was with last night said they were women who were with the Nazis."

"I wondered what happened, and if the French were really loyal to us. So what was the one you met like?"

"She was great," the soldier replied. "Brown hair, dark eyes and could speak English well enough. We met as I was walking toward one of the pubs. She was walking in a group like us, and we asked if they wanted a meal. She said yes and we went into some small pub and ate. Her husband had been killed while fighting in the French Resistance, as well as a brother, but they still had a small home on the outside of town. After we ate and talked, she took me there. She was something else. I hadn't been with a woman since before the war. I left before daylight."

Frank shook his head and said, "Well, I'm waiting until I get home. I'm still not feeling right, and I don't want to catch anything." He paused and with a serious expression said, "Then I'll have some catching up too!"

"I heard that!" said the soldier.

CHAPTER 20

Coming Home

The USS *Admiral Benson* brought PFC Frank back to the United States. The journey took about a week. The ship's ride was very smooth, unlike the trip he experienced on his deployment to Europe. Frank and many other POWs were boarded along with several thousand other U.S. soldiers. He was on the third deck below and had a bunk about three feet from the floor. Upon his arrival at his bunk, Harold looked at another former POW and said, "I ain't staying down here right now."

"Me neither," said the other, and off they went back up to the main deck.

At the same time a warning sounded, and a voice yelled, "Man your life jacket; a mine has been spotted."

Frank and several others ran up to the main deck, disobeying orders to stay by their bunks. Frank witnessed 40mm gunners firing at the floating mine. One of the POWs pulled out a German

Mauser and some ammo, and rested the rifle on the rail. Then he shot at the mine. Someone finally hit the right spot, and the mine blew up, throwing water a hundred feet into the air. Everyone cheered and a sigh of relief came over Harold. He said, "After all I've been through, imagine being blown up by a floating mine on the return home." With that he shook his head in relief.

That was the last experience of World War II for PFC Harold Frank.

This time neither Frank nor any other POWs had to pull duty or KP. Since leaving Camp Lucky Strike, the POWs had become separated, and in the excitement of returning home, they never saw each other again.

Once aboard the ship, the U.S. Army gave the liberated soldiers a hundred-dollar pay advance. PFC Frank decided during the boredom to play some poker. No one knew that Frank could play. The lessons he learned from playing poker aboard the Liberty Ship coming from New York to England in preparation for D-Day had given him the opportunity to learn the art of the bluff.

In the boredom, and after the close encounter with the mine, one of the soldiers got out of his bunk, sat on the floor, and said, "Boys, let's play a hand of poker." The soldier looked up at Frank and asked, "Can you play?"

Frank thought for a minute and said, "Why not? I'm bored just sitting here. What kind of poker is it?"

"Seven-card stud and nothing wild," the soldier answered.

"I'll try…I've only played a hand or two of what they called five-card stud."

Six soldiers sat down to play. After the first hand, Frank purposely lost. On the second hand he managed to break even but appeared confused as to how to play the game. During the third hand, he appeared aggravated. He looked at his hand: seven, nine, ten, and a jack of clubs. He discarded a five of hearts and a seven of diamonds. He drew one card, and it was an eight of clubs, giving him an inside flush of all clubs. Frank looked at the soldier with the high card who bet a hundred dollars. All except three folded, but Frank raised the bet another hundred dollars. The second man did the same and raised another hundred. The soldier with the high card raised. The soldier with the high hand looked at the two and said, "I'm going to call your bet and see who is bluffing!"

PFC Frank turned his hand over first and yelled, "I have straight-club flush, jack-high!"

The high-card man yelled, "Aw, shit! Damn! I didn't think you had much! I have a full house."

The second soldier only had three of a kind and looked at Frank and said, "You are the luckiest man I've ever seen!"

Frank laughed as he raked in the money and said, "I know it! The Depression couldn't get me. The damn Germans couldn't get me. The good Lord has been watching over me!" By the time the ship arrived in New York, Harold had over one thousand dollars.

In New York, PFC Frank was back at Camp Shanks for one
night and was issued a second round of new clothing, which Frank
packed into a duffle bag and mailed home to Tyro. Then Frank
called home to his sister Naomi and said, "I'm in New York and
being taken care of and being sent by rail to Fort Bragg."

"We'll be waiting," Naomi said.

Fort Bragg was near Fayetteville, North Carolina. He traveled all night by train and arrived at Fort Bragg on the twelfth
of June, 1945. Frank thought, "Just six weeks ago, I sat in a barn
starving to death and thinking I may never see home again."

Frank was checked out by Army doctors and given a third
set of new uniforms. A sixty-day furlough was issued, but the
war with Japan was still occurring. Frank was not discharged.
His health was better, but he refused to have pictures taken.
When the U.S. Third Army recovered him, Frank was six feet,
two inches tall and weighed a scant one hundred seventeen
pounds. On D-Day, PFC Frank was two hundred twelve pounds.
Harold was processed quickly for leave. He left for home on June
13 on a Carolina Trailway Bus with a one-hour layover in
Greensboro. At midnight, Harold arrived in Lexington.

Yates Giles had two boys and a girl who went to school
with Harold. Yates was bringing his daughter to the bus station
to head to school. He saw Harold and walked up, giving him a
hug and handshake and stating, "Welcome home! How you
getting home?"

"I'll get a cab," Frank replied.

"You're not taking a cab home. I'll bring you."

"Don't burn your gas."

"It don't matter," Mr. Giles said.

"Gas is rationed," Frank objected.

"Makes no difference. I'm taking you home, and I have plenty of gas."

After a six-mile drive at 0100 he drove up to the house driveway. Two bluetick hounds that Harold knew well came running, growling, and barking like they were going to bite him—that is, until they finally recognized him. Then they jumped up and put their paws on Harold's waist. He laughed and said, "Good boys! I'm glad to be home." Harold knocked on the door. Annie came to the door first and hollered, waking the house up. Edward Lee (Pap), Jean, and Joe (three years old) all ran to the door. "Glory Halleluiah!" was shouted, and lots of hugs and crying occurred all around. It was now one month and a week since the German sergeant told Harold to return home to his family.

Returning home was joyous to say the least, but the war left many marks. Annie cooked Harold's favorite meals, especially chicken and dumplings. For breakfast she made country ham, eggs, homemade biscuits, red-eye gravy, and homemade strawberry jelly. Edward gave the blessing, thanking the Lord that his son had made it home. But no matter how hard he tried, Frank threw up after eating. This caused concern, especially for Naomi. Uncle Pharris came to see Harold on June 14, just before dinner. Walking through the front door he saw Harold looking at Naomi and yelled, "I told you he'd be back!" Then he hugged Harold and said, "Boy, I'm glad you made it." Naomi said dinner was ready, and all sat down to feast on chicken dumplings. Suddenly, Harold left to go to the outhouse and threw up. He quickly returned and realized his family members were all worried.

"What's the matter?" they asked him.

"Nothing. I just ate too much," Harold replied.

The afternoon of June 24, Harold was greeted on the porch by his Uncle Jake, Annie's oldest brother and also a World War I veteran. Jake visited often when he was home from working for Southern Railroad, a job that usually kept him away for weeks at a time. As soon as he heard Harold was home, he came over. The two veterans walked over to the shade of the old sugar maple tree to sit and talk for several hours about war. They were both machine gunners. Harold talked about killing the rabbits and the larger German hares with the slingshot. He recalled the bits of carrots or turnips that he would steal from the animal pens to eat. Jake laughed and told Harold that near Belleau Wood in France he killed several deer with the machine gun by sending out several men to drive the deer. Then Jake opened up with the machine gun, and they ate venison.

The horror of the war memories was kept between the two world war veterans. This brought some closure, not just for Frank, but for Jake also. As the furlough time period was ending, PFC Frank telegrammed Fort Bragg for an extension. Harold knew that the fighting in the Pacific was intense, and if the war with Japan didn't end soon, he and many others would likely be called back into action. Meanwhile, Annie and Edward knew something was wrong with Harold because he continued to leave the table following meals and could be heard throwing up.

Annie would tell him, "I hope you can overcome this soon. You've got to get some meat back on those bones."

At one point Harold looked at both his parents and said, "When we were liberated, several medics told us to eat in small amounts and massage our stomachs. Guess I'll keep that up for several more days. I don't like it either."

CHAPTER 21

The Love of His Life: "Hey, Red!"

During this time President Truman ordered the atomic bombing of Hiroshima and Nagasaki. Excitement filled the Tyro community as more and more families realized that World War II was finally ending. Their sons and fathers were going to return home. On August 14, 1945, it became official as the radio and newspapers announced that Japan had surrendered. Everyone celebrated. Harold and his close friend Artis Cecil, a fellow U.S. Army veteran, joined the celebration. The two had been together in basic training with the 69th Infantry Division before PFC Frank and other BAR soldiers were removed for D-Day. Artis Cecil had been wounded twice. Now they were together celebrating in Lexington, North Carolina, on VJ Day. They stayed out all night. Once in uniform Harold received too many hugs and kisses to recollect. Harold looked at Artis and said, "I don't know about you, but I've got a lot of catching up to do!"

Several of the women who worked at the Dakota Hill Cotton Mill in Lexington dated Harold. He was excited to be home and eager to put the war far behind him. Harold went out with several of the women from the mill a few days each week. Because he knew every path and road in Davidson County, he would take them out and roam across the rural landscape. One of his favorite places was a spot along High Rock Lake not far from where he'd helped Edward and Uncle Grady mill the timber to build their homes. Before long the women from the mill villages fondly started calling Harold, "Kilroy." On a Friday night "Kilroy" Harold stayed out and went cruising through downtown Lexington. Harold pulled into a parking spot with his 1939 Ford Deluxe, which he always kept spotless and in good-running shape.

An attractive young woman came up to the window and said, "Heard about you, Kilroy!"

He couldn't help but notice the short dress and blouse she was wearing. Feeling the breeze of the summer night, he said, "Hop on in." She did, and Harold drove her to High Rock Lake. Harold turned up the radio and broke out several bottles of beer. In a few minutes they slid into the back seat and started kissing and removing clothes. Harold finally returned home around 3:00 a.m., but he threw up all over the driver's side of the car as he got out.

Edward came into Harold's room at 6:00 a.m. and grabbed Harold's foot, pulling him out of the bed.

Harold yelled, "What's the matter with you, old man! Are you half crazy?"

"Son, you come out here and look at this!" Pap yelled back.

Harold, still a little hungover, stared at the driver side of the door.

Pap said, "Aren't you ashamed of this?"

Harold paused, stood up straight, and looking at Edward said, "Yes, sir, I shouldn't have acted like that."

Edward walked over to Harold and put his hand on his shoulder and said, "Son, I know you've been through hell, but this isn't you. It's not how you were raised."

Harold saw Annie at the screen door. He nodded and said, "I know. It has been hard and a lot to try to forget. I'm sorry for worrying you and Mom."

Pap looked into Harold's eyes and said, "You better be careful and find a better choice of women."

"I know Pap, but I haven't found the perfect woman yet. I'm just not ready to settle down."

Annie, overhearing the conversation, interrupted as the two walked into the house, "Who you waiting for?"

Harold replied, "Rhonda Fleming!"

Annie laughed and said, "Well, I guess *strangers marry*." (A remark relating to a movie directed by William Castle in which actress Rhonda Fleming had a major part) With a smile Annie walked towards Harold and sat down next to Edward. Then she said, "I knew you favored redheads."

Harold said, "Well, I don't have much time before I have to report back to the Army for treatment. Maybe she'll come around afterwards."

The awkward evening out and the morning talk with his parents changed Harold. That Sunday, Harold prayed quietly during the sermon for God's forgiveness.

On August 16, 1945, Frank received orders to report to Kennedy General Hospital in Memphis, Tennessee. PFC Frank was joined by returning POWs from the Pacific. It was a big hospital. The staff told all of them that, "You all are here to recover from your POW experience. Just relax and we will help you with your recovery." Harold noticed that the returning POWs from the Pacific could hardly walk, and many were only moving via wheelchair. Harold looked at the former Army and Marine veterans standing over six feet who were barely a hundred pounds, just skin and bones. Some who were even worse had to be brought in by stretcher.

Harold confided that it was bad being in a German POW camp, but none of those survivors were in as bad of shape as those returning from the Pacific. Many of the men couldn't walk or keep food down. Most of the former POWs in Germany or in the Pacific wouldn't discuss their captivity. Harold talked with a few who had survived the Bataan Death March, and they were still just skin and bones. Many of these veterans had mental issues. They were nervous and still afraid they were going to be beaten or tortured at any time. The sudden appearance of anyone they didn't recognize often triggered a reaction. The constant issue that all shared was being unable to keep food in their stomachs. In spite of being hungry, they only ate small amounts served in a saucer plate instead of a dinner plate.

One night Harold noticed two women in civilian clothes who'd come to visit one of the Bataan Death March survivors, a man in constant pain and in a body cast in a private room. The women were trying to answer his constant request for a cigarette and whisky. On this visit he was given liquor and a cigarette. The women left the room, and not long after a fire broke out.

Harold yelled, "Fire!" and ran into the veteran's room. The veteran was immobilized in the body cast. Harold managed to pick him up, but only from the strength of the adrenaline rush, as the second lieutenant nurse grabbed two fire extinguishers. Harold picked him up, cast and all, like a block of firewood and placed him into a bed in a room across the hall. After the fire was put out, Harold looked at the nurse and said, "That was a close call."

The nurse replied, "What you did was a miracle, and I feel bad because I should've been watching more carefully." Then she walked with Harold to check on the veteran, who was okay, but unconscious.

The nurse looked at Harold and said, "Is there anything I can do for you?"

"Yes," Harold replied. "I'd like to go home for a visit, but I have no time built up and I'd be AWOL."

"You go when you like," the nurse answered, "and I'll cover for you."

Harold had a pass to leave the hospital but couldn't travel more than fifty miles. Nevertheless, with the help of the nurse, Harold traveled home six times but never for more than four consecutive days. Each time Harold told her when he was leaving and returning. Then with a parting hug he left.

One weekend PFC Frank remained in Memphis and drove from the hospital into the city looking for a date. Frank was used to a particular place, a "honky-tonk" that played only country music. He saw a woman without a date sitting by herself. He walked up and asked, "Can I have a song played for you?"

"Play whatever you want," she said.

"I know just the song," Harold replied.

He laid his infantry hat on her table and walked over to the juke box. On the way back to the table he brought two glasses of whiskey sours. She thanked him and then smiled at the tune being played, Harold's favorite. It was "The Tennessee Waltz." The two talked about their favorite songs and discovered they both liked the same music. It didn't take long before Harold realized she worked for the Army. She recognized the medals that Harold wore, and she told him that she typed many of the letters from the War Department to veteran families. She was in the women's auxiliary commonly called WACs (Women's Army Corps). They were the same age and both had grown up poor during the Great Depression. Most of the talk centered upon the war and the events surrounding the medals. She looked into Harold's eyes and stated, "In 1944 I was working in the War Department and typed up too many KIA and MIA letters to count. So sad. Excuse me for just a minute."

Harold watched as she got up and walked to the restroom. Harold paused, looking at his glass, and remembered the 357th Infantry and the men who died following D-Day. He shook his head in remembrance. Then the lady returned, and Harold listened as the juke box played, "Walking the Floor Over You" by Ernest Tubb. Harold looked at the woman and with a smile said, "You did that, didn't you?"

She smiled and sang part of the lyrics then said, "I knew you'd enjoy it."

Harold asked, "Would you like to go for a drive?"

She agreed to leave with him. They drove to a local park and talked some more. Harold turned up the country music, and the two moved to the back seat of the 1939 Ford. After the couple had finished for the night, Harold drove her to a small restaurant. The two shared a meal just before closing time. Later he drove her back to pick up her car. He walked her to her car, and as he opened the car door she said, "You take care of yourself and find you someone back home. Try to get the war behind you."

Harold looked at her and said, "Don't worry about me. A country boy will find a way to survive. Honey, you take care."

Harold kissed her goodbye and drove back to the hospital. He never could remember her name.

PFC Frank often couldn't sleep in the hospital and lay there remembering the war, the POW camp, and home. One morning, not long after dawn, Harold dressed in his uniform and walked outside the hospital. He stopped after a short distance and listening carefully said to himself, "I think I hear German." He walked a bit further, hearing it again and louder. Across the lawn he saw a group of men. Some were armed, and the others were sitting and laughing. As Frank got closer, he realized these were German POWs on a break. They looked like they were in good shape, and Harold watched as they finished eating candy bars. He couldn't take it much longer and walked past one of the MPs guarding the POWs and yelled, "You sons of bitches nearly starved me! You beat me with your rifles! You stuck me with your bayonets and executed helpless soldiers in your camps!" In anger Frank looked at the MPs and yelled, "Let me guard the Krauts!" He turned to the MP and stated, "Those German sons of bitches starved us to death and made us drink from a five-gallon bucket that was also our slop bucket!"

The MP looked at the German POWs angrily, and several other MPs came up to PFC Frank. One was a staff sergeant. He said to the MPs, "It's okay, they need to hear it."

Harold looked at the stunned POWs and yelled in German, "Why are you not working?"

One German POW looked at Harold and said, "The guards didn't seem to care and let us break."

Frank said to one MP, "Let me guard them!"

The staff sergeant motioned for Frank to come over to him. He asked Harold about the condition of the other POWs in treatment with Harold.

Harold glared at the German POWs as he answered, "We're bad off, but our boys held captive by the Japs are in pitiful shape."

Then the staff sergeant looked at Frank and said, "We've got this. They will be working digging this ditch."

Harold had one more long look at the POWs, who were all standing silently now. Then he slowly walked away.

A week later, a U.S. Army officer came into the hospital and asked for Harold Frank. The nurse took the officer to the ward where Harold was supposed to be but didn't see him there. The nurse said, "He must be in the dayroom." The two walked into the dayroom where they found Harold playing ping-pong. The two watched as Harold tried unsuccessfully to score a point.

The officer walked up and remarked, "Soldier, you haven't played this game much before?"

Harold stopped, saluted, and replied, "No, sir!"

The officer smiled and said, "As you were," and then shook Harold's hand.

The nurse promptly looked at the two and said, "Well, I'll leave you two alone."

"Thank you," said Harold.

Harold looked around and the officer walked over and said, "Your paperwork shows you're from Tyro, North Carolina. Where is that?"

Harold looked at the officer and smiled, "About halfway between Reeds and Churchland along Highway 150! That's what I told a Kraut captain after I was captured. It's really not far from Lexington."

The officer seemed to recognize the town. "PFC Frank," the officer said in a serious tone. "Your service has come to our attention. You have a Bronze Star from Normandy, but you have never formally received your Purple Heart and CIB [Combat Infantry Badge]. You were wounded on July 8, 1944."

"Yes, sir," Harold replied, and while pointing at his shoulder, he continued, "I had the round pulled from my shoulder in a POW workcamp. I still have it with me." Then he pulled the bullet from his pocket and handed it to the officer.

The officer looked it over then politely handed it back. He said, "The 90th Infantry Division has awarded your CIB with an effective date of July 10, 1944, and tomorrow during the morning formation you are going to be recognized for your actions in World War II."

Harold saluted and said, "Thank you, sir."

The officer returned the salute and said, "Thank you."

The following morning as the formation occurred the officer called out the name PFC Harold Frank. Harold broke the ranks and went forward to salute the officer. The officer read to the men the Purple Heart citation. Then he pinned the Purple Heart on Harold. He saluted and shook PFC Frank's hand. Then the officer turned to the formation and ordered attention as Harold was dismissed back to the ranks.

PFC Frank was told to reduce his meals to very small servings, which would be carefully administered with the goal of six servings per day. Then each day Frank, along with other POWs, continued participating in exercises and calisthenics. World War II was over. Harold was discharged from the hospital after Thanksgiving and told to report to Camp Butner Medical Center in Durham, North Carolina. Frank drove home in his Ford V8. The water pump went out in Murphy, North Carolina, and Frank pulled into a service station after dark. He slept until the service station opened. The owner arrived and asked, "Why are you asleep in my parking lot?"

"I'm sorry, but my water pump went out," Frank told him, "and I'm returning home from the U.S. Army Hospital in Memphis. I was in the 357th Infantry fighting in France and was captured near Beaucoudray. I was a POW for ten months and the Army sent me home before being discharged officially in Durham."

The owner nodded respectfully. He and Harold got the car into the garage, and the Ford was fixed. The owner refused to be paid even though Harold insisted.

"I will cover this," the owner said. "You have already paid the debt. Drive home safely."

PFC Frank returned home for three days and then reported to Durham where he was officially discharged from the U.S. Army on December 5, 1945.

Harold began working at Dixie Furniture in 1946. His job was on the ground floor running Salome sanding machines until the wood was smooth on both sides. One day two months after starting, Harold look out the window of the factory and saw an attractive young woman with red hair. Harold said, "Wow! She looks like Rhonda Fleming!" He whistled and yelled, "Hey!" That lasted for several weeks until one day Harold yelled, "Hey, Red!"

She turned and came up to the window, "Are you the one whistling at me?" she asked.

"Yes!" Harold replied, "Darling, can I come over and visit with you or take you on a date?"

She stared at him for a second, then said, "Come over to my house Saturday evening."

Harold said, "I'll be there at 7:00 p.m."

She smiled and replied, "I'll be waiting."

That got Harold's attention and he yelled, "Wait, I need the address."

She walked back and took a piece of paper and wrote it down for him. "Don't be late," she said as she handed it to him.

That Saturday Harold drove up in his black 1939 Ford Deluxe two-seater car with gears in the floor. He knocked, and Reba, the attractive young woman with red hair, opened the front door and invited him in. They sat down in the living room, and after a few minutes he asked, "I'd like to ask you out, to go to a movie in Winston."

"You will have to get permission from my dad," she replied.

Harold, somewhat surprised, found her father in the kitchen and asked him, "Can I take Reba to the movies in Winston-Salem?"

"I reckon it will be all right," Mr. McDaniel said.

"There is no 'reckon,'" Harold replied. "I will bring her back just like she is now."

"You think you're tough?" Mr. McDaniel asked.

"No, but the damned Germans couldn't kill me. Have I got permission?"

"Yes."

"If I have to ask permission each time, I won't be coming back."

"You have permission and won't need to ask again." Mr. McDaniel answered.

Harold assured Reba's dad, "Don't worry. I will take care of her and not take advantage."

He told Harold, "If she tells me she is all right, you won't need to ask again."

At the movies, Harold and Reba kissed. On the way home, they stopped at a drive-in with curbside service. The two had their first dinner and ordered a BLT sandwich and Coca-Cola. They ate while listening to the Grand Ole Opry. Reba asked, "What happened in the war?"

Harold, still skinny and trying to recover from POW treatment, said, "I don't want to talk about it right now. Maybe one day in the future I'll tell you all of my story, but not now. I got wounded and captured, but I made it back and that's what's important."

Reba smiled and said, "Okay," and never brought it up again.

Harold was impressed with her country upbringing, Southern voice, and the way she loved country music. She could sing many country tunes by heart.

On their next date, Reba asked, "Would you like to hear some country music?

Harold said, "Yes."

Reba played Ernest Tubb's "Walking the Floor Over You." With its Philco automatic changer, the 78-speed record player began to play, but instead of just listening to Ernest Tubb, Harold heard the most amazing alto voice sing the song word for word along with it. Roy Acuff 's "The Precious Jewel" came up next.

Harold and Reba dated Saturday, Sunday, and Wednesday nights. They also saw each other at work at Dixie Furniture. Harold would open the door for her to get into the car. The first time she said, "I can get in without help."

Harold replied, "I don't mind. It's what I want to do."

She liked that.

One day after the two had been dating for several weeks, Harold picked her up as usual. As the two drove away, Harold had the radio on the Grand Ole Opry, "WSJS Nashville." Reba began singing, "The Tennessee Waltz" in a voice never to be forgotten. A year back now, Harold remembered the loneliness of Klotzsche Airfield POW work camp and the consolation provided by the Delmore brother with the borrowed guitar playing "The Tennessee Waltz" as the POWs tried to sleep. Harold looked over at Reba and began to sing with her. He knew he had found the love of his life.

Harold did manage to fulfill a wish of Edward's. The Great Depression created extreme poverty for so many people, but one of the pleasures Harold's family enjoyed was sitting together each Saturday and listening to the Grand Ole Opry. In October 1946, Harold got tickets from Reynolds Tobacco Company for the Red Foley Show and took his dad to Nashville. They all loved seeing the Grand Ole Opry "live." They stayed in the Opry house from 8:00 p.m. till 11:30 p.m. Roy Acuff, Ernest Tubb, and Eddie Arnold were the main stars. Ernest Tubb concluded with, "Walking the Floor Over You."

Afterwards, the family drove to the edge of Nashville and stayed in a motel. They were thrilled, and Harold said, "Pap, hope you enjoyed the Opry."

Edward looked at Harold and said, "Best show in the world. I'll never forget this."

"By the way Pap, I may have found the right woman. She even looks like Rhonda Fleming."

"Good, son, can't wait to meet her. Have you told Annie?"

"Not yet, but I will before long," said Harold.

Soon after getting back from the Opry, any concerns that Harold may have had about Reba ended with one meal. Reba was a member of the Cornatzer Methodist Church and invited Harold to a box supper. At the church each person had to buy a box with a prepared meal that was unmarked to keep the buyer from knowing the owner. Reba cheated by telling Harold which box was hers so he would buy it. Harold got into a bidding war with another man. Harold was beginning to get upset but finally outbid the other man. The two took the box and found a table. Harold took one bite and couldn't believe how good the food was. "This is better chicken dumplings than my mom can fix." Harold knew from that point on he would never go hungry.

Soon after Harold proposed to Reba. He was preparing to drive back to Davidson County after dropping her off from a date.

Harold looked at Reba and said, "Darling, I've been burning up the road between Davie and Davidson Counties long enough. Will you marry me?"

Without hesitation she said, "Yes."

The two kissed, and she ran into the house with excitement. The couple had been dating for a year and decided the wedding would be October 11, 1947. It would not be a large wedding or a honeymoon vacation. Harold worked hard at Dixie Furniture, and as he prepared for the wedding, he began putting more of his salary away to find and obtain furniture for an apartment. Survivors of the Depression typically believed that any money gained should be saved. Harold was saving so he could get a nice place for them to live. Harold married Reba Mae McDaniel on October 11 at Tyro in the Saint Luke's Lutheran Church parsonage at 5:00 p.m. Saturday evening. Afterwards, the newlyweds had a dinner prepared by Annie Frank. Then Harold took Reba to his new apartment in Lexington five blocks from where the two worked. After a night of bliss with little sleep, the couple returned to work.

The only time Harold thought he might lose Reba, the love of his life, was in January of 1948. Harold and Reba were invited to a Sunday dinner at his boyhood home. It was an outstanding roast beef dinner. Reba went to help Annie in the kitchen with the plates.

Harold said, "I'm going to run into town and visit my friends that I haven't seen since the war ended. I won't be gone long."

Annie looked at Harold and said, "Be careful."

Reba looked at Harold with a suspicious gaze.

Harold instantly repeated, "I won't be gone long," and left.

Harold arrived at Leonard's Sawmill. The owner allowed the group of men to play poker there. Six men counting Harold arrived. One looked up and said, "Kilroy, you made it back. Have a seat and we'll deal you in."

"What are we playing?" Harold replied.

"Five-card stud," the men said.

Harold played two hands and ended up making just a little change. Then he thought, "What is Reba thinking?" From that point Harold had problems concentrating and began losing. After ten hours, Harold looked up and said, "Boys, I've got to go. I've been here too long already." A few handshakes followed, then Harold was out the door and driving home.

Annie and Reba were in the kitchen. Edward had gone to bed. Annie looked directly into Harold's eyes. "Son, where have you been? We've been worried."

Harold replied, "Nothing to worry about. I was just out with the boys."

Reba looked at Harold sternly and said, "Are you ready to go back to the apartment?"

"Yeah, let's go," Harold replied.

In the car Reba was quiet for several minutes. Harold looked over at Reba and said, "I'm glad you didn't get onto me in front of Momma. If you had chewed me out, I would've been mad."

Reba looked at Harold and said, "I know you've been playing poker. Well, there is one thing about it. You can either have me or the poker game but not both."

Harold sat and thought about it for a while. Then he looked at Reba and said, "I can do without the poker game, but I can't do without you."

Reba politely nodded but remained quiet for the rest of the drive home. True to his word, Harold never went back to Leonard's Sawmill in Tyro.

CHAPTER 22

Thanks for the Memories

In 1948 Harold left Dixie Furniture for a much higher-paying position at R. J. Reynolds Tobacco Company. Harold and Reba didn't like living in town, and Otis Hendricks, who admired Harold's work ethic, offered to sell them a house and a small farm of sixteen acres not far from Reba Mae's family. Harold bought the property and moved to his new farm in Davie County, North Carolina. With all the love and care the two shared together, Harold finally recovered from the war and could finally eat a full meal without becoming sick. However, the final paperwork to receive all the back pay from his POW experience came with a shock. Harold came home from work, stopped at the mailbox, and found a letter from the Army. The letter thanked him for his service. Then it continued to inform him that he would receive the POW bonus pay for all but five days—the days he had escaped. He paused in disbelief. For those five days he would receive regular pay. Harold saw Reba and said, "Read this," and handed her the letter. She looked shocked as she read the letter. Harold said, "I was in more danger during that time than while captured."

Reba looked at Harold and with a serious tone said, "Harold don't get upset over this."

"Well, I can't help it. They're docking me five days' pay, and I thought each day I would get killed." Harold decided not to pursue the matter and never received the extra five dollars.

In November of 1949, Harold's home was twenty miles from Edward and Annie. Harold's phone rang and Reba answered, "Hello."

Annie was on the other end and said, "I need to talk with Harold."

Harold took the phone and asked, "What is wrong?"

"Something is wrong with your Dad. He is losing his mind. I've called your Uncle Pharris and he is on the way."

Harold and Reba left, and when they arrived Pap was standing in the wheat field with his bulldog. Uncle Pharris arrived and yelled to Harold. "You get the dog, and I'll get Ed if he falls or runs."

Harold got the dog as he walked up to Edward and said, 'Pap, are you ok?"

Pap looked at Harold and said, "Time to get the horse teams together and meet Uncle Grady at the mill site."

Harold looked at Uncle Pharris and then back at Pap, replying, "Nelle and Gray were still eating. Let's walk back and give 'em a few more minutes."

"We need to go soon; I've got to get the houses built," Pap replied.

By the time the ambulance arrived, Edward didn't recognize anyone or understand what was happening. After being loaded into the ambulance he became incoherent.

Reba leaned over Edward, trying to wake him, and calmly called out, "Edward . . . Edward. It's Reba, can you hear me?"

Edward's eyes opened. He looked up and saw Reba and focused on the necklace she wore around her neck. It was a gold chain that Harold had bought. Reba had Harold's Purple Heart fastened to it and wore it every day. It was dangling down from her chest. Edward became composed and slowly but clearly opened his eyes and said, "Reba!"—that's what he had always called her—and began to point towards Harold and continued, "Take care of him because my son went through hell to get it."

Reba looked at Harold with her eyes beginning to water and said, "I will."

Then Edward fell back asleep. He died later in the Lexington Hospital on Valentine's Day.

Years later Annie's health declined, and her daughter Jean moved in with Annie to help her. Annie developed Alzheimer's disease and deteriorated. Archie was Annie's power of attorney because he lived close by her house. One day he called Harold and said, "Mom is unable to care of herself. Jean is doing what she can, but Mom doesn't know where she is or when to go to the bathroom."

All the family got together at the home place and agreed to
send Annie to a rest home near Lexington, North Carolina.
Within a few months, Annie was unable to recognize any of her
children. She passed away at the age of ninety-four. It was a
peaceful funeral. Harold walked up alone to her casket and said,
"Mom, I love you and I know you are better off. I hate that I
worried you so much during the war. It was your prayers that
kept me alive." Tears came from Harold's eyes, and he concluded, "You're home with Pap. We'll all see each other again,
and it'll be a happy day just like when I came home from the
war." Harold put his hand on Annie's hand and said, "I love you
and I'll see you again." Pulling a handkerchief from his pocket
he wiped the tears from his face and cheek as he walked out of
the funeral home. Reba hugged Harold, and putting put her arm
through his, they walked to their car and waited on Annie's
casket to be loaded into the hearse. She was laid to rest beside
Edward at the Sandy Creek Lutheran Cemetery.

Harold Frank began working for the Davie County Sheriff's
Office under Sheriff George Smith. In all Harold would work as
a special deputy for twenty-four years under four different sheriffs.
As a special deputy, he was asked to provide security at the local
Farmington Drag Car Speedway, high school events, barn dances,
and especially the Crosby Golf Invitational Tournament held
every year in nearby Bermuda Run. Sheriff Smith asked Harold
to serve as the personal security at the Bermuda Run Clubhouse.
After his first year, Harold left an impression and was asked to
accompany celebrities as security while they played. It was his job

to keep members of the audience from running up to the celebrities and distracting them.

Before World War II, Harold knew Bob Hope as a movie star and radio comedian. Hope's affiliation with the USO was widely respected by many servicemen. Harold was never able to see Bob Hope while in the service, but Hope's dedication to all who served appealed to him. Any of the Bob Hope shows that appeared on TV was a special occasion. Harold and Reba would watch with anticipation. Most Americans grew to enjoy the humor and entertainment of the shows. For Harold, it became a way to remember those he served with during World War II. It was also a connection to war memories that he kept private. Reba seemed to understand this connection and would sit close to Harold and hold his hand. In her own way, Reba would raise a laugh from Harold by saying, "You just want to see which actresses are going to appear on the stage with him." Jane Russell, Raquel Welch, and Ann-Margret were attractive to Harold. However, Harold's favorite actress had always been Rhonda Fleming. Harold would affectionately tell Reba, "You're my Rhonda Fleming, and I wouldn't have it any other way."

Reba would say, "I'm not that pretty."

Harold knew she only said that to hear him say, "You're more attractive than her in my book."

When Bob Hope came to the Crosby Invitational Tournament, Harold became part of his security detail. Harold was thrilled! Harold noticed that the comedian was easy to like. The soldier in him brought the two men close. Harold made sure to keep the crowd back, and Bob Hope took note. Although he appreciated the attention to detail with crowd control, Bob enjoyed trying to speak with everyone. Harold recalled a funny incident in one of the tournaments:

"We were on the front nine of the golf course. Hope was about to move up on the fairway, when a lady with her two sons ran up. I stopped the three and told the lady, 'You're not supposed to be here during this round of golf.'

"Hope interrupted and said, 'It's all right. I'll make my picture with them.'

"The lady asked, 'Please let me snap a picture of you with my two sons.'"

Harold noticed with a smile that the boys were small, perhaps six to eight years old. As the lady was snapping the picture, Harold looked at Bob and pointed to the lady's camera. She was beginning to walk away, and Bob Hope stopped her. Then he said, "Do it over, you didn't have your lens cap off when you took the picture."

She looked embarrassed and laughed before taking a second picture.

As the tournament ended, Harold escorted Bob Hope to the clubhouse door. Before going inside, Hope stopped and asked Harold, "You haven't asked for my autograph."

Harold replied, "I'm not supposed to ask for an autograph or bother you in any way."

Bob Hope reached out and took off Harold's golf tournament security cap. Then he pulled out a pen from his pocket, signed the cap, and placed it back on Harold's head.

Harold said, "Thank you for the memories!"

The comment brought laughter from people walking into the clubhouse.

Harold continued to work for R. J. Reynolds Company in Winston-Salem. He retired in June 1982. Harold remained a Davie County Sheriff's Deputy for several more years. He retired from the Sheriff's Office in 1985, leaving athletic events, the Farmington Drag Strip, and high school dances for someone else. Harold finally returned to only working a farm in 1988. He and Reba now had more time, and they enjoyed traveling together across the nation.

In November of 1987, Davie County placed a memorial to veterans across from the courthouse. Harold Frank was a member of the Veterans of Foreign War and by 1987 was an elected officer. He worked with all the local chapters to raise funds to pay for the monument. Local hero and bombardier on the Enola Gay, Thomas Ferebee, had a brother who was a close friend of Harold Frank. At the ceremony crew members of the famous B-29 bomber were present, including Pilot Paul Tibbits, and Bombardier Thomas Ferebee, whose farm was in Davie County. Harold Frank was in the group photo. He talked with Thomas, who was standing close by his brother Bill.

Not long after the event ended, Harold and Reba were eating dinner when the phone rang. Reba answered and handed the phone to Harold. William Ferebee called and asked if Harold could come by the Ferebee home place. That weekend Harold went to visit, and Bill Ferebee showed him the largest registered bluetick hound dogs that Harold had ever seen. Bill invited Harold inside and wanted to talk about the war. At that time Harold rarely went into an in-depth discussion about his experience. This was an exception. The friendship grew, and Bill and Harold continued to discourse over farming and war stories.

On March 16, 2000, Colonel Thomas Ferebee died at his home in Florida. At the request of the legendary bombardier, his body was taken back to Davie County, North Carolina, to be buried at his boyhood Methodist church. Harold and Reba received an invitation to the funeral. Harold and Reba arrived with the crowd of several hundred. The funeral procession left from the funeral home in Mocksville. The line of cars stretched for miles and arrived at the cemetery near Farmington, North Carolina. It was a military funeral accompanied by a U.S. Military Honor Guard. As taps were being played, Reba put her arm in Harold's and held tight. From the sky a roar could be heard, and in a short time a U.S. Air Force B-1 Bomber came over from the west low in the sky. It made a circle. When it flew over the second time the B-1 turned the nose up and hammered the bomber into full speed. With a deafening sound it disappeared into the horizon. All cheered at the tribute to one of America's greatest heroes. Reba looked up at Harold and said, "He saved a lot of lives. Had he not dropped that bomb, you and millions of other soldiers could've died invading Japan." Fighting back tears, Reba held Harold's hand and said, "You'll always be my hero. I love you." Then the two kissed and walked back to their gold 1972 Buick Limited car with a 455 V8. After exiting the church and with open road before him, Harold let the V8 roar as another veteran's salute.

After retirement, Harold was invited to fish off the coast of the North Carolina Outer Banks in 1990 with Roby Joe, his youngest brother. Harold constantly joked about Roby Joe, claiming, "I had to change his diapers all the time." Roby Joe had purchased a twenty-foot, twin-engine Grady-White fishing boat and loved the North Carolina Coast. The first trip was near Hatteras Island, where they caught their limit of croakers. The brothers became hooked on fishing. Every October the two brothers would leave to fish. Roby Joe eventually bought a home in Sunset Beach, North Carolina. Brother Archie began accompanying the two after the third year. For the brothers, it was a chance to catch up after years of hard work and relative separation. Although in the decline of old age, times were better for these brothers from America's Greatest Generation. They no longer needed to make their own fishing net to catch bait fish. Now the brothers went to a local bait store on Hatteras and purchased the casting net, fishing reels, eyes for the rod, and fishing line. However, one day Harold returned home and, true to his upbringing, returned to the woods. He found a hickory tree that was long, straight, and just big enough to become a fishing surf rod eight feet long. Harold took the tree into his workshop and peeled the bark, sanded it smooth, and covered the wood with wooden shellac. He fastened the rod onto a two-by-four by driving nails on each side of the pole to keep it straight. Every ten inches he bent a nail over the rod. After two months the pole cured. Harold used a pocketknife to carefully cut the spots for each eye that the string would run through. He carefully wrapped each eye connection in tight fishing line, and then covered the whole rod with shellac. Afterwards the reel was mounted to the rod and prepared for fishing. There is no doubt that a blend of American ingenuity combined with new technology made for a damn good fishing rod.

On the next fishing trip Harold brought out his homemade fishing rod, and the brothers shook their heads. They said, "It's too heavy for fishing."

Harold replied, "That's what y'all think! It won't break!"

The brothers took off from a small inlet near Topsail Beach, North Carolina, and commenced to fish. While looking across the blue water, Harold reflected on his past. He thought of the lessons he learned living through the Great Depression and all the hard work in the cotton patch with Naomi. Although Edward had passed, he could still hear his voice, "You think you can handle the horse teams when you're eight?" Harold smiled and then reflected on PFC Paul Esworthy and the men of the 357th Infantry. He thought about the misery of the POW experience combined with the horrors of war that constantly haunted the quiet but seldom idle moments in Harold's life. Fishing brought calm to his nightmares. On this day, looking out over the ocean, it brought peace.

The brothers seemed to understand Harold and rarely brought up the war. The Grady-White slowed down as they arrived at the fishing hole that Roby Joe had preselected. The boat's captain maneuvered the boat for the fishermen. Once the boat stopped, they looked at Harold and said, "Kilroy! Time to fish!" In a few minutes Archie hooked a flounder. Roby Joe finished maneuvering the boat and joined his brothers fishing. Before long Roby Joe landed a flounder.

Harold looked and said, "Y'all are getting too close to me!" He cast again and felt a bite. Harold jerked the rod to set the hook and felt the pole pulling down hard. Reeling quickly he worked the rod up and down.

The brothers laughed and said, "Hold onto it! Now we will see what that rod can do!"

In a few minutes, Harold pulled to the surface a beautiful, ten-pound bluefish. Harold grinned and said, "I warned you about talking about my damn pole! It's larger and stronger than yours!"

Roby Joe laughed, and Archie patted Harold on the back and said, "That's a nice fish."

At night they would play some poker and laugh while remembering the Depression, World War II, and hard work. During the day, fishing meant business, and for Harold, the fish of choice was flounder. Roby Joe loved speckled trout but agreed with Harold that flounder was good eating. As soon as boat captain Roby Joe saw the brothers ready to throw in their lines, he looked at Harold and repeated their time-honored ritual call, "Kilroy, time to fish!" The brothers never missed a trip until 2008.

In 2008, Reba's health began to decline. She was diagnosed with macular degeneration. Harold stayed by her side and stopped making the fishing trips. Within two years she was diagnosed with type 2 diabetes. Harold cared for his wife every day, refusing to leave her side. Even at death, Reba respected Harold's request not to talk to her about the war. This time she looked at Harold with her limited vision and while holding his hand said, "I hope you will one day tell your story."

Reba, the love of Harold's life for over sixty-eight years, passed away on January 21, 2016. After Reba's death, Harold felt compelled to make his story known. Many nights he wakes up and reaches for her, still thinking she is there. He can still hear her alto voice singing, "The Tennessee Waltz."

CHAPTER 23

A Day to Remember

Three months after Reba's death, and completely by chance, Harold and I met at a local farm luncheon sponsored by Spurgeon Foster. The Foster family had recently purchased the historic Cooleemee Plantation and its two thousand acres of farmland. As president of the Forks of the Yadkin and Davie County History Museum, I was assisting Spurgeon Foster in interpretative ideas as well as advising the current preservation operations on how to restore the grounds. Arriving late at the luncheon, I went through the buffet line quickly and looked for an empty seat. While gazing across the room and saying hello to local residents, I glanced to my right and noticed a POW cap and an empty seat. As a U.S. Army veteran, I look for fellow veterans. I ate a wonderful lunch and asked the veteran sitting next to me his name and branch of service.

"PFC Harold Frank, U.S. Army, World War II."

I was stunned and asked, "What unit did you serve with?"

"I went through basic at Camp Shelby, Mississippi with the 271st Infantry in the 69th Division but landed in France with 357th Infantry in the 90th Division," he told me.

I interrupted and asked this veteran, "You were with the 357th at Utah Beach, the 357th that was virtually wiped out in the Cotentin Peninsula?"

With a short laugh and a characteristic shake of the head, Harold replied, "We lost a lot of men."

I paused, remembering the many World War I and II veterans in my own family, including a cousin on the USS *Pennsylvania* at Pearl Harbor, an uncle that landed at Anzio and fought into France before being wounded, a great uncle who fought as a machine gunner during World War I, and many others. Reading military history, historic reenacting, military service, and teaching public history are inspirational. Now sitting beside me was a man whose survival in France—not to mention his still being with us today—would shock most World War II historians.

I looked at Harold and said, "I was in the Army and stationed for a while in Germany. I saw some of the places where you would've fought. Can I ask you some questions?"

He said, "Yes," and I looked for something to write on. All I had was a napkin and a few business cards. Harold asked, "You've heard of the 357th?

"Yes, sir, part of the 90th Division 'Tough Hombres,' but I've never talked with a member of that regiment. You guys went through hell in Gourbesville, Beaucoudray, and Saint-Lô."

Harold interrupted, "Yes, we did!" He shook his head and his eyes watered. "I was wounded one month after Utah Beach near Beaucoudray and was captured. I hid my wound because they executed the wounded man beside me. He was shot in the leg and couldn't walk. I was shot in the shoulder."

"Where were you taken as a POW?" I asked Harold.

"Near Dresden," he replied.

I responded, "You were at the city firebombed by the Eighth Air Force in 1945?" I have to admit I was speechless. I was thinking, "Why have I never heard of Harold Frank and how is he alive?"

After everyone else had eaten and left, we kept talking until I ran out of cards to write on. Harold said, "Would you like to come over and hear the whole story?"

"Yes, sir, how close by do you live?" I asked.

"Just a few miles," and he turned toward Spurgeon Foster, laughing, and stated, "He can get you to my place."

I walked over to Spurgeon and said, "Thank you. The food was outstanding. Also that man's survival is a story people need to hear. There can't be many, if any, survivors from his company or regiment."

Spurgeon replied, "I know it. He really hasn't opened up about his war experience until after his wife died."

The first day I arrived on his farm with pen and paper ready, I met Harold's son Eddie, who was a Navy veteran. Eddie said, "He will be here in a minute. He's spreading manure in the pasture."

I asked, "He is ninety-two and still able to do work like that?"

"Oh, just a few weeks ago he had the chain saw out cutting trees," Eddie replied with a serious tone.

Harold arrived and walked over to shake my hand, and I immediately asked, "What's your secret to staying healthy?"

Harold grinned and said, "I don't drink no sodas, because everyone that does has health problems."

"So what do you drink?" I asked.

Harold replied, "Water from my house, whole milk, and two teaspoons of 100 percent apple cider vinegar per day. Don't matter the brand. Get the cheapest one."

I laughed while shaking his hand and said, "That's all? Nothing else?"

Harold paused and chuckled. "Well, a sip of applejack or corn whiskey for medicinal reasons." He smiled and said, "When I get a headache, a sore throat, it'll clean your system out!"

Harold does have some arthritis from a knee wound during the landing on Utah Beach. He rubs apple cider vinegar on it each night to stop the pain. The only medicine he takes is a daily vitamin pill that a doctor prescribed for his vision.

As we began to talk, Harold mentioned that he told people some of his war memories and one article was published in the local *Davie County Enterprise Record*. It was entitled, "To Hell and Back." It was never the full and complete history that I am humbly honored to write about. In the process I produced a documentary on part of his story called *From B.A.R to P.O.W.:*

The Harold Frank Story. The documentary became widely viewed in the community and was on UNC.TV during the spring of 2017. One of the proudest moments of this work was my showcasing of the documentary at a veterans' coffee event hosted by Richard Childress at his NASCAR facility in Harold's original hometown of Welcome, North Carolina. Don Timmons, a Vietnam veteran and hospice chaplain, organized the coffee and asked that I show the documentary. It was an honor and tribute to all who have served this nation. I was asked afterwards if Harold could speak at the Memorial Weekend Coca-Cola 600 pre-race chapel service for the drivers and their teams. Harold without hesitation said, "Yes!" The next week my phone rang, and MRO Racing asked if Harold would give the invocation before the flyover and national anthem, to which Harold again replied, "Yes!" I told him to speak to the drivers for five minutes and that his prayer could not go longer than twenty-six seconds. Harold replied, "I can do it because you're going to help me." It was a daunting task that in the end proved to be unforgettable. I thank Richard Childress, RCR Racing and NASCAR for their attention and respect to all our armed forces.

In the chapel service, Harold Frank underscored and challenged the teams to keep prayer in their daily lives. He explained that as a BAR Rifleman he excelled in the 271st Infantry Regiment and could disassemble and assemble the weapon blindfolded in ten minutes. Harold stated, "If you take care of the weapon, it will take care of you." Likewise, he told the teams, "If you work hard, know the equipment, and keep prayer in your life, you'll do well." When he said that, I thought, "There is always Edward, and especially Uncle Pharris, speaking again through Harold." Harold finished by telling the crowd, "Never give up and always keep going. Take that next step even if you think you can't." While the chapel service continued, renowned sketch artist Jared Emerson completed a painting based upon a photograph that I had given to him of Harold Frank during World War II. The following was PFC Harold Frank's message to the drivers at the Coca-Cola 600:

> I think it is a great honor to be asked to talk with this group of NASCAR drivers and employees. I was raised in a Christian home, and we were members of Saint Luke's Lutheran Church in Tyro, NC. We seldom missed a Sunday service and even though it was the depression, we tithed and helped the members in any way. My mom gave me this New Testament when I went to World War II. It was all I had to read while fighting and then as a POW. In World War II, I was a BAR Rifleman, which was a .30–06, and there was only one in each infantry squad and the only automatic rifle in each squad. It could fire several hundred rounds per minute, and I volunteered to carry it. It was the only time I ever volunteered. My platoon sergeant, Sergeant Friday, told me if I took care of it, it would take care of me. After a few months, I could disassemble and put it back together

blindfolded in ten minutes and qualified best in the whole regiment, the 271st Infantry Regiment at Camp Shelby, Mississippi. Likewise, each of you here is part of a team where trust and hard work go hand in hand. Place prayer in your daily life, and if you know the equipment it will take care of you.

I prayed before every battle and, if possible, on a Sunday attended a short prayer meeting with the Army Chaplain. Most Sundays, however, following landing on Utah Beach, we were in full combat. After landing on Utah Beach I fought non-stop for thirty-one days. During the fighting at Beaucoudray, I was placed in a patrol because I was the last experienced BAR Rifleman. We were trying to locate two lost U.S. Army companies. We didn't know that at the same time the 15th German Parachute Regiment launched a major counterattack. Shortly after daylight I was shot in the shoulder and fought nine hours before being captured. The Germans executed a fellow soldier I was trying to help. His leg had been fractured and couldn't walk. I later found out that my assistant gunner PFC Esworthy wasn't captured but died from wounds at the battle of Saint-Lô a month later.

Following capture and interrogation, I prayed every night for God to save to my life. I also prayed for my mom. I knew no matter the circumstances that she was praying for me, and I felt her prayers. She didn't know if I was alive or dead for several months. Then, she received a letter that I was a POW. I never told mom or dad that I had been wounded, starving losing over ninety pounds in captivity. They would have worried even more. I prayed that I would survive the war and return home.

I saw things most people should never see. On February 12 and 13, American and British Bombers attacked Dresden, Germany. Our POW camp was just outside of the city, and I saw German military equipment heading to fight the Russians. Our bombers destroyed the city, and some one hundred thousand people were killed—but the POW camp survived. So I know that if you never lose faith in God and your country, you can make it home safe. Never stop praying, work as a team, and remember the cost of freedom.

In conclusion Harold paused from reading the speech and looked at the audience and said, "When you get to that point when you're tired, exhausted, or don't know what's next and think 'I can't take another step.' Just put that foot forward and take another step and then another. You'll pull through. Don't never give up!"

At the invocation Harold brought the crowd of one hundred thousand to their feet and with a loud cheer he addressed them, "Thank God I'm an American! Let us all pray." His prayer was larger than the Coca-Cola 600 and was meant for all Americans:

> Thank you, dear Lord for all of your many blessings and for saving my life. Lord, bless our military for without our armed forces we would not have the freedom we cherish. Keep them safe and return them to their families. Lord, be with the drivers and their teams today. Guide them through this race and along with the fans gathered here in Charlotte I pray that all return home safely tonight. Thank you for the freedom we all share as Americans. In Jesus' name I pray. Amen."

After that the national anthem was sung, and a squadron of F-15 fighters roared overhead. The prayer and the anthem were timed perfectly. In the stands, the infield, and on the track, not a single person was sitting. Harold gazed and reflected on his service and the memory of the real heroes, those who never came home because they gave the ultimate sacrifice, their lives.

The race was dedicated to U.S. soldiers who gave their lives for freedom and liberty. Strangely enough, lightning delayed the conclusion of the race. The winning car had near impossible odds of winning. The number three car of RCR Racing driven by Austin Dillon crossed the finish line first—against all odds and out of gas. Before the race RCR changed the paint scheme and added a proudly displayed U.S. Flag decal. Due to the weather, the final laps of the race had to be run after midnight, making it Memorial Day. The team RCR defeated was team Toyota. All I can possibly add is, "God Bless the U.S.A."

CHAPTER 24

Until We Meet Again: Soaring Valor

The National WWII Museum in New Orleans became acquainted with both Harold and I due to a Soaring Valor Flight back in August of 2018. The Gary Sinise Foundation sponsored the special flights which were to bring the last remaining veterans of World War II to the museum to watch the popular documentary, *Beyond All Boundaries*. This was the museum's latest documentary on World War II, produced by actor Tom Hanks, directed by David Briggs and shown in 4D. Gary Sinise is best remembered in Hollywood productions such as *Forrest Gump*, where he played the character of Lieutenant Dan. I remembered the important role Gary Sinise played in the movie *Apollo 13* where he played the role of NASA astronaut Ken Mattingly. Sinise has always had a deep desire to help our nation's veterans. Sinise proudly remembers his two uncles who served in World War II, and after the passing of his Uncle Jack, who was a navigator on a B-17 that flew thirty missions in Europe, Sinise began a partnership with the National WWII Museum. Sinise developed the Soaring Valor Flights program, which fits well with the foundation's mission: To ensure the sacrifices of America's defenders and their families are never forgotten.

Harold left a lasting impression on the museum staff as well as the foundation. I spoke with the National WWII Museum president Stephen Watson about the documentary I had completed on Harold in 2017. It was the first attempt to document and share Harold's story with friends, family, and residents in North Carolina. We are appreciative for the dedication of the National WWII Museum and all its staff in preserving the stories of the Greatest Generation. I was particularly amazed at the patience the staff had in both listening to and recording the memories of veterans. We knew collecting memories from individuals well into their nineties and trying to piece the collections into a timeline was a daunting task. It was especially difficult for veterans who spent most of their post-war years trying to erase much of that memory. Watson echoed the sentiment that it is important to record the memory of these remaining few while we can. I agreed.

Just before we left to return for North Carolina, several of the museum staff informed me that they were going to attempt a last large gathering of Normandy Campaign World War II veterans in France for the 75th anniversary of D-Day.

Watson asked, "If it happens, would you be able to get Harold to travel?"

I told them that Harold has been asked several times before but turned it down with the usual answer: "I went one time, and never wanted to return. I don't want to get stuck again."

However, I told the staff, "This time, especially after this Soaring Valor trip, I think he may." I smiled and looked at Stephen and mentioned, "If you tell him that the Victory Belles will be there, the chances would be really good." That created a good laugh among the staff.

Stephen Watson shook my hand and said, "I'll be in touch."

After returning to North Carolina, Harold came by my museum office, as he frequently does now. I told Harold of the possibility of the 75th anniversary trip and that it might be the last attempt for a large gathering. Harold looked at me and said, "There getting to be fewer and fewer of us. We were once sixteen million but now maybe a few thousand." Late that January 2019, I received a call from the National WWII Museum that the trip would be happening, and they would be sending the information. I called Harold a week later and he came to the office.

"Well, Harold," I asked, "will you go this time? It may be the last chance."

Harold paused and said, "I'll talk it over with the family, but I think I will."

Harold had a heart problem requiring the placement of a stint to ease a clot issue. That operation became the key for the trip. As it turned out, Harold pulled through easily. He came back to my office and said he would go, but he wanted me to go with him.

"It would be an honor, but we need to get you in better shape to handle the ten-day travel event. The itinerary begins with flying to Amsterdam, then going by cruise ship to several different ports across Belgium, France, and England. It will culminate with the 75th Anniversary Ceremony at Sainte-Mère Église. It's a lot, but if you're up to it, I would be honored to travel with you and try my best to keep you out of trouble. By the way, the Victory Belles will be with us."

Harold smiled and said, "Oh, Lordy! Don't worry about me, I'll be ready. A country boy knows how to survive."

A few days later, he purchased a stationary bike, rearranged his living room, and worked daily to build up his strength. I was impressed at the change in Harold. By the end of May 2019, he was ready.

My son-in-law had a day off from the police department and volunteered to drive both Harold and me to the Greensboro International Airport. The National WWII Museum had already purchased the coach tickets on United Airlines. As soon as the two of us made it to the ticket counter, people came over to greet us. Harold as usual had his medals hanging from his dog tags, which were fastened to a gold chain. United Airlines employees immediately offered assistance and without any protest brought up a wheelchair for Harold. Along the way to the gate, a security officer with his K-9 approached. He asked to shake Harold's hand, and as usual Harold said, "Yes."

"Where did you serve?" the officer asked Harold.

The reply was quick, "In World War II. I was with the 90th Infantry Division after they arrived on Utah Beach. Saw my first combat near dark somewhere near Gourbesville, France. Somewhere near Beaucoudray I was on a night patrol trying to locate two companies that had got separated or overrun. After daybreak I was shot in the shoulder by this round. It stayed in my shoulder for several months until a German doctor cut it out while I was a POW near Dresden."

The office ordered his K-9 to sit and said, "Can I sit with you for a while? It would be a real honor."

"By all means," Harold replied.

The officer asked what we were going to do.

Harold looked over and pointed to me and stated, "Ask Mark, he's been really good to me and helped put me on the map."

I laughed and spoke with the officer. "Harold had been selected by the National WWII Museum along with several other Normandy Campaign veterans to travel for what they believe will be the last large attempt to gather survivors of D-Day and the Normandy Campaign."

The officer looked at Harold and asked, "Have you ever gone back since the war?"

Harold thought and looked toward the United Airlines gate. "No. To tell you the truth, I never wanted to go back." With tears in his eyes, he continued, "I went once before and like to have never made it back home. I saw things I wanted to forget that no one should ever have to see. I was shot in the shoulder, captured, and put in a Nazi POW Camp for ten months. I survived it somehow." Then he looked at the officer and said, "If it hadn't been for my momma's prayers, I couldn't have made it back and I know it."

I tapped Harold on the shoulder and said, "What led you to change your mind this time?"

"Well," Harold said, "I went to the World War II Museum in New Orleans, sponsored by the Gary Sinise Foundation. It was a wonderful trip. Mark introduced me to many people; that included the president of the museum. They told me they were going to try to make this trip happen and it may be the last time. My wife that I was married to for sixty-eight years wanted me to tell my war story, but I told her no. After she passed away last year, I decided to try to tell it the best that I could remember. Anyway I had a good trip, and told Mark if they can arrange it, I'll go back this time. I wanted Mark to go with me because he has a way of getting me to see the right people and places I wouldn't know how. Even though he drives a Chevy truck instead of a Ford, he's all right."

I shook my head and looked at the officer, "He asked me to go, and I told him it would be an honor. Even then I thought, if this is the last large gathering, I need to record this for history. I managed to purchase equipment that was light enough and easy to carry but also able to record in 4k."

The officer said, "I'm glad to have met you all." He reached out to shake Harold's hand.

Harold said, "It's good to meet you, and keep the place safe."

The officer laughed and replied, "You be careful and don't fall down."

I immediately chimed in, "He's used to walking. He drives a Ford!"

Harold laughed and motioned at me with his fist. Together we all walked toward the airport gate arguing about Fords and Chevys.

As we prepared to board the United Airlines flight, I thought about all that was awaiting us. We would begin in the Netherlands and travel by a cruise ship, *The Regent Navigator*, to various ports across France and finally to England. After a month of trying, we couldn't raise the funds or make the logistics work to bring Pritchett Cotten, a close friend and exceptional videographer. I told Pritchett, "You're going to have to train me on the new equipment, and then we'll put it all together after we get back." I had some working knowledge of photography and film due to work in public history. Pritchett was an excellent coach, and I took many notes. In fact I made three sets of identical notes on color-coded index cards. Then I took pictures with my cellphone and stored them on my laptop. I had practiced for several days before the trip and stored the index cards for quick referral. My goal was to video the whole trip and cover the individual stories of other World War II veterans, especially those joining us from North Carolina. I took out my Panasonic G4 DSLR and asked if I could get a picture of the K-9 Officer. The officer said, "You sure can." That officially marked the beginning of the 75th Anniversary of D-Day experience.

Once onboard the flight, I told one of the stewardesses, "Traveling with me is a member of the Greatest Generation and a Normandy Campaign veteran."

She looked over at Harold and said, "Oh, wow! We were told that we may see some heading to Europe." She gave Harold one of many hugs that would follow on the flight. We had just started towards our seats when she called us back and said, "You two follow me." We moved around some of the passengers to get back to her. She said, "I told the captain about you two. You all have been upgraded to first class."

Harold and I looked up, and he said, "Can't beat that," as we arrived at our upgraded seats. Other United Airlines attendants came over to meet Harold and took pictures with him. After a few minutes, the captain came on the speaker and announced, "Today it is an honor that traveling with us is a World War II veteran who fought in the Normandy Campaign and is going to the 75th Anniversary of D-Day Ceremony. Please join me and welcome him as our honored guest." We could immediately hear loud cheers echoing well outside of the first-class area. Neither of us realized it yet, but this exuberant mood would grow as the trip continued. I laughed as a group of attractive United Airlines flight attendants gathered around Harold to show him how to work the seat controls and the movie selections. I knew he couldn't hear most of what they were explaining and that he was more interested in all the hugs and attention. Since it was a long flight, they tried to show him the list of movies and scrolled through several screens.

At one point Harold looked up and said, "Don't y'all have something with John Wayne?" They all looked at each other then back to the screen.

One of the stewardesses said, "I don't see one, but here is Clint Eastwood. Have you seen *Unforgiven*?"

Harold said, "Yes, ma'am, and that'll do."

She walked over to me and said, "I just love that man!"

Once Harold was comfortable and quiet, I looked over and said, "I wonder what Pap and Annie are thinking?"

"Oh, Lordy!" replied Harold. With a grin he said, "Pap would've said, 'Boy you ain't got any sense.'"

At Flanders Field—We Remembered the Fallen

Our first tour was away from the war experience. Once aboard the cruise liner *The Regent Navigator*, Harold felt right at home, especially when the National WWII Museum's trio known as the Victory Belles appeared. Harold could always spot the most attractive women with or without his glasses. He especially looked for any with auburn or red hair. One of the Victory Belles fit that image. It must run in the family because Annie, Reba, and his favorite movie star, Rhonda Fleming all had red hair. Upon seeing Harold, the Victory Belles rushed over and gave him big hugs. I could hear Harold laughing and saying, "Thank you, darlin'," to each one. I knew this would be a very special trip as long as he didn't overdo it. "Where are the Belles?" was the reply every time we arrived back on the ship. Most of the women Harold met throughout this trip couldn't get enough of him.

Windmills of Kinderdijk—May 29–30

We traveled by bus to see the Windmills of Kinderdijk. It was an amazing scene and a peaceful way to begin this trip. The tour guide brought us through Rotterdam. We stopped to walk around the port where the *Speedwell* and its Pilgrim passengers originally began their voyage to the New World. Harold tried to listen to the tour guide but had hearing-aid issues and said, "Tell me what she said later. I'll stay here looking over the canal." The windmills together with the picturesque canal were a sight never to be forgotten. Harold decided to rest on a bench and take in the scenery while I ventured into the windmills to film and photograph how they operated. When I walked out, I noticed that Harold already had an audience. Traveling with us were several members of the King and Brushy Creek Ranches in Texas. They noticed the dog tags and medals that Harold kept around his neck ever since the war. With camera in hand, my documentation of the trip continued. They asked Harold where he was going next, and Harold said, "You'll have to ask my manager!" He pointed at me. I told them we were going to the World War I Museum in Ypres, Zeebrugge, and Flanders Field. They asked to join us and learn more about the story of Harold. This created a bond that continues to this day.

Laying the Wreath at Flanders Field

After we had originally boarded the *Regent*, we also met Stephen Watson who was expecting to hear the two of us arguing about trucks. He saw Harold and said, "I've got a Chevy truck waiting to tour you around New Orleans."

Harold laughed and said, "Not if I can help it."

Nearby a Medal of Honor recipient approached the three of us. Harold noticed the medal adorning his neck and reached out to shake his hand.

Stephen Watson introduced him by stating, "This is Britt Slabinski, retired Navy SEAL that completed several tours in the Middle East."

Harold said, "It's an honor to meet you."

Slabinski stated, "Same here. I'll be joining you all on many of the tours."

The following day we traveled to Flanders Field. Everyone was solemn upon seeing the carefully manicured grounds dotted by so many World War I American graves. Harold and I walked around and tried to locate fallen soldiers from North Carolina. It didn't take long to locate others, like in all wars, who fought and died still in their youth. The director of the site came by and heard Harold say, "Freedom isn't cheap. Someone has to pay the price." The director noticed the medals on Harold and asked if he would help with the "Laying the Wreath Ceremony" for the American Cemetery, which happened to be that day. I had to repeat the question closer to Harold's hearing aid, and before I could finish, he turned and said, "I sure would." At the main memorial, Harold was joined by Britt Slabinski. Minutes later a minister approached as visitors had already gathered for the event. Scriptures were read. The minister prayed. Then he asked everyone to pray again in silence and remember the fallen. After prayer the group laid the wreath, saluted the memorial, and stood at attention as taps played. It was a memory that no one would ever forget.

Afterwards, Harold and Britt continued to talk about their service. Harold told him about battles around Normandy, and Britt talked about Afghanistan. They were two decorated American soldiers remembering the men who didn't come back. Both agreed that those who did not return were the real heroes. Harold looked at Britt and mentioned, "You know, I got the French Legion of Honor last year in Charlotte. They told me I could only wear it on a uniform."

Slablinski, looked seriously at Harold and said, "If they have already awarded it to you, it doesn't matter now. Wear it whenever you want to. The men that fought beside you would expect you to."

Harold paused, looked up and said, "You're right. I think I will."

Colin Taylor and the Raid on Dieppe Tour

Harold didn't want to go on this tour at first. Then there was something about the tour guide that caught his attention.

Harold Frank receives the French Legion of Honor in Charlotte, 2016

His passion for World War II caused Harold to look at me and say, "He says it the way he should and doesn't hold back anything. Let's go on this tour." I have to admit, I was hoping to go on the tour. In my Army service I was stationed in Germany during the 1980s. I had heard and read about this attack but didn't have the opportunity to visit the site. I remembered the raid as a suicide mission that thousands of Canadian soldiers never returned from. Most people today, including military veterans, have little knowledge of this raid. The actual raid caused a rethinking of how the Allies would eventually attack two years later for D-Day. There were five beaches each with their own objectives. The invasion attempt would be a combination of air support and infantry assault along with armor floated in for support. As guide Colin Taylor pointed out about the Raid on Dieppe, nothing worked as planned. The lay of the land and the planning were flawed and doomed from the beginning. Harold and I looked around the beach and giant cliffs that were referred to as "the casino." Both of us shook our heads in disbelief. Harold looked at Colin and said, "It looks impossible for any attack to have ever worked here." Harold paused, and looking out at the cliffs above the beach, said, "I just don't think they knew how strong the German soldiers were here along this beach.

I replied, "Bet the Germans were dumbfounded why anyone would attack this spot."

Colin Taylor remarked, "It was a failure and terrible price that was paid. It also was a lesson for the Allies if they were to ever try it again. They would, but not before two years of planning. They needed to get the logistics right. They had to provide complete air support and be sure that tanks, trucks, and reinforcements would be continuous. Then it could be done but not here, nor at any major port city."

Harold shook his head and said, "Those boys had no idea what was going to happen. They had no chance."

Later the bus took us to the outskirts of town along the picturesque French countryside. Greeting us were the graves of the men killed in the Raid on Dieppe.

As we approached the cemetery, Harold wanted to sit and view the grounds from the bench near the gate. I continued into the cemetery with Colin Taylor but asked him, "Would anyone be offended if I stood on the cemetery wall to take a panoramic picture of the graves?"

"I think they would be honored that you are remembering them," Taylor replied.

I walked up and couldn't believe the sight of so many young soldiers who perished on the unintended suicide mission. Colin and I walked and took pictures of individual graves marking the different Canadian soldiers and units. One that I pointed at seemed out of place and caught my attention. Colin walked over and said, "Some of the men in the attack were French soldiers that fought here as commandos. One that was captured was ordered to take the French insignia off his uniform." I looked at Taylor, as he continued in a somber tone, "France had surrendered and was now a German proxy. If those commandos didn't take the French flag off their uniform, they were shot. Here is the grave of one unknown French commando. He refused to take his nation's flag off his uniform."

I looked at the grave and thought about "Old Glory." I paused, and as I took photographs I told Taylor, "That's a price that was paid for freedom and a distinct honor for all generations to see." Trying to hold back emotion, I stared at the grave and said, "All veterans should see this."

"You have the camera."

"That I do," I replied.

Unknown French Commando from Dieppe Raid, August 19, 1942.

The Battlefield Tour with Mark Hager and Sylvain Kast

Harold didn't realize it, but before final trip preparations I talked with the National WWII Museum about taking him on a special private tour of the battles in which he had fought. In the weeks before the trip, we located local Normandy historians and looked into the logistics of how to make such an event happen. The tour guide we decided upon was Sylvain Kast. His family was from the area, and one of his family members fought in the French Resistance during World War II. His devotion to soldiers who fought to liberate France was incredible. His ability to communicate with Harold and his knowledge of the ground triggered

Harold to recover much of the memory he had previously erased. Moreover, Sylvain was able to make sense of the combat experience that had been suddenly thrust upon the young Harold. Harold was able to recall events upon seeing the hedgerows. There were the railroad tracks where he had helped capture seventeen German soldiers. Then he suddenly remembered the truck ride from Utah beach. In tears he recalled spending two nights on the beach before he and PFC Paul Estworthy were ordered into the truck. The truck moved a short distance through Sainte Mère Église and dropped them off at the 90th Infantry Division rendezvous point, which looks similar today but, of course, without all the death. Harold remembered the dead cattle that he and Paul saw as they moved forward to join the 357th Infantry headed toward Gourbesville. He explained in detail seeing gliders with men still dead inside and trees with U.S. Airborne parachutes fluttering in the wind, some with dead soldiers still attached—sadly, a memory no one would want to keep. Many questions were finally answered. Harold told us about becoming a replacement and joining a unit in which he knew no one, except for Paul. Then he was suddenly locked in desperate combat. He didn't know the names of the towns, villages, or rivers. He just wanted to stay alive, protect the men around him, and come home. Needless to say, much emotion would be shed on this trip. The climax of the personal tour would be the church near Beaucoudray where Harold was wounded and captured.

When we arrived at the church the expectation of being on the battlefield where he was wounded and captured made him forget about his bodily functions. After getting out of the car, Harold pulled Sylvain away and asked, "Where can I go to the bathroom and let out some water?"

Sylvain laughed and said, "You just go right over there across from the church and relieve yourself in the hedgerow."

Harold shook his head and said, "Never took a leak outside a church before!"

Sylvain replied, "I think the Lord will understand."

Walking to the back of the church, Sylvain asked, "Harold, do you feel better?"

Harold just laughed and said, "I hope the good Lord will forgive me."

In a compassionate tone, Sylvain said, "Come over here towards the wall. As you walk, look at the grave markers in this area. You can see the bullet and shrapnel damage still to this day. It was this battle in which you and the men that made it across the road fought. Here are the effects today."

Harold walked slowly, studying the ground. He carefully made his way to the wall. Sylvain pointed out across the field beyond the cemetery and said, "Around the group of trees was where the foxholes were that you must have been in when you were shot. Most likely a German sniper was in the tree because the church steeple had already been blown apart."

Harold paused, tears in his eyes, and looked across the field. He finally said, "The Lord has been good to me, and I know it. How I survived this had to be God's call. My momma did a lot of praying, and He answered her."

Both Sylvain and I gave Harold a hug and stood silently as Harold continued to gaze across the field. I told Harold, "You just remain here, and we will give you as much time as you need to think. I will photograph the graveyard battlefield damage and come back."

Harold said, "Thank you. I hope you know how much this trip has meant to me. I couldn't have done it without you."

"It's an honor and pleasure," I replied.

I walked into the graveyard with Sylvain and noticed that his eyes were watering. I paused and said, "You brought back an understanding of his battlefield experience. Before this trip I feel he had a lot of confusion about the combat he experienced and how he moved from the beach to join the 357th Infantry. He had been removed from his division, the 69th Infantry at Camp Shelby, and thrust into this conflict. He only knew one name, PFC Paul Esworthy. By the time the 357th was here at Beaucoudray, most of the veterans were also replacements."

Sylvain replied, "I think the heaviest fighting that the 90th Division, 357th Infantry faced during the whole war was between Gourbesville and Beaucoudray. They faced heavy artillery, machine gun, multiple panzer attacks, as well as hand-to-hand combat day and night."

I paused and turned to take a few pictures of Harold near the wall and Sylvain called out, "Mark, did you notice the bullet and shrapnel scars on the tombstones?" I looked down and positioned the camera and took pictures of each one. Then,

Sylvain pointed at a piece of shrapnel in part of the rock wall. I took photographs and suddenly it dawned on me.

I looked at Sylvain and said, "On the trip here, Harold remembered being in a truck leaving Utah Beach and it was on that trip that he saw the German artillery inside a French home. That's where he began to remember what happened. The rendezvous site of the 90th Infantry Division was the place he was off-loaded with Esworthy on the way by foot to Gourbesville. That is where he saw the airborne soldiers still hanging from parachutes in the trees and the gliders with American soldiers killed upon impact. Your knowledge has finally given closure. He knows the reason for why

75th Anniversary of D-Day—Rifle fire fragments from the Battle of Beaucoudray on a tombstone

and where he was. He also knows the events that eventually led to his wounding and capture at this location." I patted Sylvain's shoulder and said, "Before this trip, it was a horrible nightmare of jumbled sets of combat events and night patrols, followed by ten months in a Nazi POW camp. His only concern was getting back home to Annie and Pap. Dates, time, and places were of little concern to PFC Harold Frank. He was just trying to survive so he could see home again. Most civilians and families of combat veterans can't understand." I shook my head, then added, "You have a talent to see through this and place the memories in the right perspective." When we returned to Harold, I asked, "Are you ready to head back to the boat?"

Harold replied, "Yes, I think so."

From that point on we could see the relief on Harold's face. Finally it all made sense.

June 6, 2019—75th Anniversary of D-Day Ceremony

June 6, 2019, began with lots of excitement. Harold was treated by the ship's crew with breakfast in bed. Scrambled eggs, bacon, waffle, mixed fruit, and coffee, plus a glass of orange juice. By 9:00 a.m. we all headed from the ship to tour buses lined up to head to Sainte Mère Église. The weather was cool and overcast with a temperature of fifty-eight degrees. Unlike the other trips, this one was definitely unique. French police and local security lined up to escort the buses. They did a superb job, redirecting traffic so that the buses carrying

75th Anniversary of D-Day—90th Infantry Division Memorial, Utah Beach

World War II veterans left unimpeded. There was lots of laughter onboard the bus that carried Harold. World War II veterans discussed the events over the past few days. Harold and James Deal reminisced about farm life and how beautiful the French farms were.

Harold commented, "Looks so much different than in 1944. Back then, there were dead cows and destroyed villages dotting the countryside. A terrible waste of fine farm animals."

James replied, "But just look at it now. It's wonderful. So different."

I looked over and heard the loud ringing of Harold's hearing aids and asked if he needed them adjusted.

Harold responded, "What?" Several repeated the question to Harold. He looked up and said, "What I need is to have my ears cleaned."

James Deal's granddaughter Jordan asked, "How do you clean your ears?"

Harold cupped his hand around his ear and said, "Repeat that again?"

"How do you clean your ears?" Jordan yelled.

"Usually have it washed out," Harold replied. "But sometimes I use a bobby pin."

I put down the camera and looked at both Harold and James. I shook my head and said, "You do what?"

James interrupted and said, "I do the same thing. A bobby pin works wonderful in getting that wax build up out. You know what I mean?"

Lots of laughter occurred across the bus with several World War II veterans nodding in agreement. One person yelled out, "Kinda dangerous during a thunderstorm, too much to worry over during a lightning strike."

James and Harold laughed and responded, "That's right!"

The 82nd Airborne Division became the personal entourage for the World War II veterans. Everyone had nothing but praise for each veteran. Getting the veterans to the stage was a huge feat to achieve. The crowd size was easily half a million. Many that I spoke with felt that this could be the last gathering. Pondering that thought, I realized that if this were tried again for the eightieth anniversary, the youngest veteran would be ninety-nine. We noticed all who had gathered for this event were excited. Crowds moved out of the way and clapped as the veterans were escorted to the stage. Countless numbers wanted to shake hands and, when possible, give hugs. At one point, Harold looked over at me and said, "This is wonderful, but I've shaken more hands today than in ninety-five years combined."

The World War II veterans were taken to assigned seats. All were to be together, as they should. The rest of us were placed in rows farther back on the stage. I thought, "Harold is separated once again but this time to honor and remember those that never came back." In front of the stage and behind the audience lay the graves of over nine thousand American soldiers. The white crosses and Stars of David dotted the green landscape right down to the blue Normandy beaches. The sight brings chills to me just remembering it. Key points came in phrases. President Macron turned at one point and clearly but solemnly stated in English, "We know what we owe to you, veterans." Then he paused and looked at the veterans and said, "Our freedom, thank you."

Later President Trump stirred the emotions with his statement, "To the men who sit behind me and to the boys that rest in the field before me, your example will never ever grow old. You're among the greatest Americans who will ever live. You are the pride of the nation. You are the glory of the Republic. Thank you from the bottom of our hearts."

Immediately all stood and cheered and clapped to thank the men who defeated tyranny and restored freedom. Afterwards the French Airforce gave a patriotic flyover that was joined by planes from World War II. For at least thirty minutes the sky roared with military aircraft, just a small taste of the sounds seventy-five years earlier. Then, the two presidents turned to shake hands with the veterans.

As President Trump walked over toward Harold, shaking the hands of each World War II veteran, Harold reached out his hand. President Trump grabbed his hand and looked at Harold.

Then President Trump said, "Thank you."

Harold looked directly at the president while grasping his hand and said, "Keep up the good work."

President Trump paused and replied, "Thank you."

Then Harold shook the hand of Melania and said, "Take good care of Donald. We need him for eight years."

"I'll try to take care of him," Melania said.

Normandy Cemetery

As we all left the stage and walked by the cemetery, Harold said, "Just look at the numbers of crosses and Stars of David." He continued, "I didn't think I could ever go back. How I could have fought, been a POW, and made it home? During that time, I didn't think I would ever see home. After getting home, I always thought, freedom isn't free. Someone has to pay the bill. I wanted to make something of myself. Every day is another day that the boys in the cemetery never had. I've always had a job. No matter my condition or health. If I quit a job, I had another already lined up. Because when you give up, it's over. Like going to court and pleading guilty but knowing you never did anything wrong, and no one even accused me of doing anything. I just walked in and said, 'throw me in prison.' That's what it's like to be a quitter. It would be more than letting myself down. It would be letting my Pap and Momma down. And most of all, it would let all the boys who never returned from the war down. Why anyone chooses to prefer prison is beyond me. That's why I wanted to return for the 75th anniversary. I felt it was going to be the last large gathering of us, the boys that fought in Normandy. I owe it to all the boys buried here to return and see them one last time. I'm not perfect by any means, but I've tried to do my best. What could I say to them? What would I tell PFC Esworthy if I could? I'm sorry for being captured and not being there with you at Saint-Lô. We may have survived together. But I don't know."

As we prepared to leave, I put Harold in a wheelchair. I could tell that this event was finally draining away a portion of the energy he had worked hard to build up. I told him, "Let's just stroll through the cemetery. This time in peace."

Harold said, "Right on!"

As we went by row after row of graves, I stopped and pointed out a grave from a soldier who was in the 90th Infantry Division, 358th Infantry Regiment. I said, "It's not the 357th but they were right beside you. Would you like to get out and see it?"

"Yes, I would." Harold got up and walked into the cemetery.

I remained at the edge of the row and said, "Let me hold your cane. You go and be with them." I watched as he walked out, and carefully paused, to salute the grave of the 90th Infantrymen. Then I could see he was talking, but this time only to them. Then he gazed over many acres of the fallen just to remember all he could. He walked out beside me stopped and turned around. He gazed over the men resting and said, "Until we meet again."

Harold's Fear

Harold Frank worries more than ever that today the new generation of Americans are forgetting not only the cost of freedom and liberty but also the faith and determination of our past citizens. In Frank's day Americans came up in the Depression mostly poor. "We killed small birds, squirrels, turtles, opossums, and other animals to find the food we needed. All we knew was how to farm and work hard to make every cent to stay alive. Even though I was injured at Utah Beach, wounded at Beaucoudray, I survived ten months in captivity at a Nazi prison camp, and couldn't eat right for ten years. More importantly, every day, and especially in the stillness of night, the memories of war come. The smells, sounds, screams, and horrible sights never go away. Regardless, I came home and worked. If I left a job, I already had another prepared. The memories of war are always with me, but I didn't let it bring me down. I'm not perfect, but I've kept a faith in God, which like many in my generation helped create exceptional soldiers and leaders. I wonder about this generation."

After listening and writing the story of Harold Frank, a couple of questions come to mind: Has this generation lost the initiative because so much has been handed down to them causing a loss of ingenuity and faith? Also, if the United States is ever attacked, would people know what to do or how to survive like Harold was able to do in World War II? Or will many give up? Reba asked Harold about the war when they were dating. He didn't want to talk about the war then. Out of respect and devotion, so as not to reveal the real horror of war, he told her no and maybe sometime later. After sixty-eight years of marriage, the love of his life passed away, and only then did he feel ready to share his remembrances, not just with me but with a nation that he feels is in trouble.

Naomi died a few years before Reba after a long illness on July 19, 2012. She lived a long life of ninety years working and residing near Lexington, North Carolina, and had two children. Harold's brother Archie served in the Merchant Marines and the U.S. Navy as an electrician. After the military he worked as an electrician and is still residing in Tyro, North Carolina. Melba Jean never married and remained close to her mother. On June 26, 2014, she was tragically killed in a car accident while on a trip to Myrtle Beach, South Carolina. Roby Joe went to school to become a welder and worked on the transcontinental oil pipeline in Houston, Texas, before returning to Lexington to start his own welding company. He is retired and still resides in Lexington, North Carolina. The three brothers enjoyed fishing with each other until four years ago when Reba's health went into decline. Since then age and energy have taken a toll. Harold still misses the fishing trips off Hatteras Island with his brothers. PFC Paul Esworthy fought on with Company G to Saint-Lô. It was there that he was severely wounded and taken to England where he succumbed to the injury. His body was taken back to his family, and he is buried at the family church cemetery near Frederick, Maryland. Harold never made contact with the three other POWs who had become a team and together survived the ten long months of a Nazi work camp. Like many of his wartime memories, Harold kept them shelved for a later time. It is without doubt that Reba saved Harold and revised his priorities.

Each Christmas, Harold drives out to Reba's grave, opens the door on his Ford pick-up truck, and plays her favorite Christmas song, Bing Crosby's "I'm Dreaming of a White Christmas." Fighting back tears while the song echoes loudly across the cemetery, he sits and remembers what nearly a century of incredible experiences can create. Afterwards, he tells Reba goodbye. Then closing the door and wiping back a few tears, Harold drives back home as a ninety-six-year-old combat veteran in his white Ford pickup truck. On the back window, a decal reads: "WWII Veteran."

Notes

Chapter 6:
Faith, Sports, Walter Winchell, and That Damn T-Model

1. Franklin D. Roosevelt, "Fireside Chat," September 9, 1939, Online by Gerhard Peters and John T. Woolley, The American Presidency Project, https://www.presidency.ucsb.edu/node/209990
2. Franklin D. Roosevelt, "Address to Congress requesting a declaration of war," December 8, 1941, Library of Congress, https://www.loc.gov/item/afccal000483.

Chapter 10:
D-Day to Gourbesville: Rendezvous with the 357th Infantry

1. Dwight D. Eisenhower, "D-Day Statement to the Soldiers, Sailors and Airmen of the Allied Expeditionary Force," June 6, 1944, National Archives, https://catalog.archives.gov/id/186473.
2. Franklin D. Roosevelt, "Prayer on D-Day," June 6, 1944, Internet Archive, https://archive.org/details/FdrsPrayerOnD-dayJune61944.

Index